Return to Me

says the Lord

Return to Me says the Lord

"A Journey of First Love Surrender"

Gregory Reed Frizzell

Return to Me says the Lord: A Journey of First Love Surrender
ISBN 978-1-930285-95-8
Copyright © 2012 by Gregory R, Frizzell
Published by Master Design Publishing
    789 State Route 94 E., Fulton, KY 42041
    www.masterdesign.org

Additional copies of this and other books by Dr. Frizzell may
be
ordered from:
Baptist General Convention of Oklahoma
3800 N. May Ave., Oklahoma City, OK 73112-6505
phone: 405.942.3800 e-mail: gfrizzell@bgco.org
or online at www.masterdesign.org

All Scripture Quotations, unless otherwise indicated, are taken
from the New King James Version of the Bible, copyright ©
1982 by Thomas Nelson, Inc. Used by permission. All rights
reserved.

Cover Artwork

Cover artwork 42436277 ©MozZz-Fotolia.com

Additional Resources Available from Dr. Frizzell

Returning to Holiness *A Personal and Church-wide Journey to Revival*

How to Develop A Powerful Prayer Life *The Biblical Path to Holiness and Relationship with God*

Local Associations and United Prayer *Keys To The Coming Revival*

Biblical Patterns for Powerful Church Prayer Meetings *God's Changeless Path to Sweeping Revival and Evangelism*

Prayer Evangelism for the Local Church *One Church's Miraculous Story of Blessing and Deliverance*

Seeking the Reviver, Not Just Revival *Personal and Corporate Prayers That Bring Sweeping Revival*

Building an Evangelistic, Kingdom-Focused Church Prayer Ministry *God's Path to Revival, Discipleship and Evangelism*

Holiness and Power in Christian Leaders *A Leader's Life Journey of Cleansing, Revival and Spiritual Intimacy with God*

Powerful Marriage and Family Prayer *Restoring the Missing Key to Healthy Families and Revived Churches*

Saved, Certain and Transformed *Journey to Biblical Salvation, Full Assurance and Personal Revival*

Dynamic Church Prayer Meetings *Why Every Church Must Embrace Them!*

Empower Us O God *A Leader's Preparation for Acts 1:8 Evangelism, Ministry and Prayer*

Seeking God To Seek A Pastor *Vital Steps for Search Committees and Congregations*

Perfect Peace *How to Never Again Doubt Your Salvation*

Sunday School, Small Groups and Kingdom Prayer *The Dawning of a Revival Revolution*

Miraculous Church Unity and Kingdom Vision *Journey to Biblical Fellowship and Revival*

Iceberg Dead Ahead *The Urgency Call to God-Seeking Repentance*

Forty Days of Seeking God *Praying for Revival, Elections and Key Leaders*

How to Pray Without Ceasing *The Power of Continuous Talking and Listening to God*

Praying God's Heart in Times Like These *Co-Laboring With God to Turn the Tide of Darkness*

How to Conduct a Solemn Assembly *Leading Congregations into God's Manifest Presence*

Powerful Church Unity and Kingdom Vision *Overcoming the Disunity that Grieves God's Spirit*

Clean Hands and Pure Hearts *Victory Over Impurity, Pornography and Wrong Relationships*

The Fullness and Power of the Holy Spirit *Restoring the Missing Key to Victorious Life and Service*

Upcoming New Releases

Abiding in Christ *Dynamic Daily Prayer and Intimacy with Christ*

In Remembrance of Me *Developing Lord's Suppers that Change Churches*

Restoring the New Testament, Great Awakening Church *The Seven Priority Practices of Empowered Churches*

Demolishing Personal and Church-wide Strongholds *Spiritual Warfare that Releases Revival*

America — Revival, Judgment or Both? *Recognizing and Reversing the Twenty-five Devastating Signs of the Times*

The Call to Holiness Online *Keeping Blogs, Emails and Tweets from Going Too Far*

To Schedule Church or Region-wide Conferences

For information concerning conferences or resources contact
Dr. Frizzell at:
Baptist General Convention of Oklahoma
3800 N. May Ave., Oklahoma City, OK 73112-6506
phone: 405.942.3800 e-mail: gfrizzell@bgco.org

Conference Titles

➤ **Turning Pastor Search Into Church-wide Renewal**

➤ **"Going Deeper With God Weekend"**

➤ **Developing Mountain-Moving Prayer and Intimacy with God**

➤ **Journey to Holiness, Joy and Power**

➤ **Church and Association-wide Revivals and Solemn Assemblies**

➤ **Transformed Relationships, Healed Families and United Churches**

➤ **Holiness and Power in Christian Leaders**

➤ **Developing Powerful Prayer Meetings and Evangelistic Prayer Ministries**

➤ **Building Dynamic Marriage and Family Prayer**

➤ **Biblical and Historic Patterns of Spiritual Awakening**

➤ **Saved, Certain and Transformed**

➤ **Seeking God To Seek A Pastor**

Table of Content

Introduction

Returning to God in First Love Surrender

Welcome to a journey of full surrender and renewal in Christ! If you are weary of praying for renewal in your life or family without seeing it, you are not alone. Be assured, God has promised a path for victory! If you yearn for more of God's blessing and power in your life or church, there is grace for a whole new beginning. Though this book is a journey of deeper surrender and cleansing, it is even more about renewed closeness and New Testament power in Jesus. And while at some points God will bring conviction, He convicts to *transform* not condemn.

In a day when many believers lack victory, we will together experience a journey of God-seeking surrender. Through God's grace, believers will learn to experience long-sought breakthroughs in their lives and families. (2 Corinthians 2:14; Philippians 4:13) In so doing, God receives greater glory and Christ's kingdom expands in power. He is glorified when we bear much fruit through prayers that have power! (John 15:7-8) Even if society continues to spiral downward under greater judgments, God's people can still be revived!

Concerning this book's title, some may wonder why they need to "return to God." According to Scripture, all believers need periodic times of deeper cleansing, commitment and growth. In Zechariah 1:3, God extends a glorious invitation and promise. *"Return to Me and I will return to you says the Lord."* The Bible is filled with examples of God calling His people to new vitality through deeper surrender. (2 Chronicles 7:14; Joel 2:12-18; James 4:8-10) Yet today, many efforts at cleansing are so general and surface, they are not a genuine return to God. This book is about a full lasting return to first love surrender.

Recognizing Today's Extreme Spiritual Urgency

Collapsing Morals and Growing Crises

In the fall of 2007, I released the pilot version of **Iceberg Dead Ahead:** *The Urgency of God Seeking Repentance.* The book highlighted the extreme urgency of societal conditions and strong likelihood of coming shocks. The timing was very significant as just four months later, America experienced a series of devastating economic, societal and spiritual icebergs.

As we near the release of the expanded **Iceberg Dead Ahead**, conditions are again showing significant signs of escalation. There are strong indications we could soon see worsening judgment in our land. Regardless of who is in the White House, worsening economic, moral and spiritual icebergs are dead in our path. With a catastrophic deficit, growing cyber-terrorists, geo-political threats and fast worsening persecution, there is an unprecedented need for revival in God's people! Yet sadly, many believers are unprepared to be God's light in the growing darkness of our day.

Studies leave no doubt that alarming numbers of churches lack biblical vitality and power. More and more Christian parents are seeing their children ripped away from their faith as soon as they reach eighteen. In rapid fashion, this shocking pattern has exploded to between 70 and 80 percent! Rather than being God's answer to a world in turmoil, many believers are themselves being decimated by worldly influences. Sadly, many Christian leaders have pinned their hopes on some new method or relational technique to turn the tide and reach society.

Methods Alone are *Never* God's Main Answer
(2 Chronicles 7:14; Mark 11:17; Acts 1:8)

While a flood of new strategies have been proclaimed as the primary answers, we must recapture the following eternal truth. "Methods and techniques alone are *never* God's main answer for sweeping spiritual awakening." Troubling numbers of growth theories either seriously marginalize or wholly ignore fervent prayer and God-seeking repentance. Sadly much church growth theory is more about location, style and watered-down preaching than deep repentance and biblical discipleship.

As a result, too much of today's "evangelism" is yielding more *surface decisions* than *genuine converts*. Today's appallingly low baptism ratios are in stark contrast to both the New Testament and historic awakenings. Yet, there is hope! Some of today's new strategies are truly excellent and a small remnant is beginning to seek God in a whole new level of prayer. Beyond question, you *can* be a part of that committed remnant!

How to Best Use This Tool
"Practical Options for Believers and Churches"

First, some believers may choose to simply pray through the twenty-one day journey on their own. On each day, they will experience deep cleansing and focused biblical prayer for personal renewal and revival in our land. Over the twenty-one days, participants will pray through specific Scriptures that address every area of life. Without embracing *full* yielding, a powerful move of God is virtually impossible. (Psalm 66:18;

James 4:8-10) In **Return to Me**, participants will experience life-changing yielding to Christ.

Second, believers are encouraged to fast from at least one meal daily (or weekly) during the twenty-one day emphasis. They should spend that meal-time praying through some or all of the biblical prayers compiled in Appendices D and E. (The prayers are for lost people, missions and spiritual awakening.)[1] These two appendices contain biblical prayers for revival, awakening and lost people in a concise list. The prayer guides are available as Bible inserts for powerful ongoing use *after* the twenty-one day emphasis.

Third, congregations should seriously consider conducting a solemn assembly or powerful church-wide prayer meeting on the Sunday that concludes the three week emphasis. In most cases, the church leadership will plan and conduct this special service. The book, **How to Conduct a Solemn Assembly** is available from the office of Prayer and Spiritual Awakening. We also provide free down loadable materials for believers and churches. In addition to following a biblical pattern for Spirit-guided solemn assemblies, it is often helpful to have *responsive reading* covenants for specific prayer and surrender to God. (Our website provides these.)

Fourth, at the end of the twenty-one days embrace **My Covenant to Return to God** (which is fully outlined in Appendix A).[2] The covenant includes a set of five Bible inserts to equip believers to live out their new surrender to Christ. Through these Spirit-guided steps, daily victory can finally become a reality! Saints, if all we do is a general "cleansing emphasis" (without specific steps for lasting change), a full return to God is virtually impossible.

At the back of the book, readers will find an implementation tool entitled, **My Covenant to Return to God.** It consists of five Bible inserts to help any believer walk in lasting victory. These practical tools help modern believers recapture the essential patterns for lasting change.

Through these practical tools they learn to (1) embrace continual first love passion for Jesus, (2) experience deep daily cleansing and power, (3) pray much more effectively, (4) pray for salvations, missions and deliverance in lost people and loved ones, (5) pray for revival and spiritual awakening. While believers are certainly not required to do all five every day, even once or twice a week can revolutionize their lives! Best of all, these biblical tools are simple, easy to use and totally centered in God's grace.

Trust God for a Life-Changing Encounter

(Jeremiah 33:3; James 1:5)

Readers who have worked through our book, **Forty Days of Seeking God** will notice some similarities in **Return to Me.** However, there are some meaningful differences and this is a more condensed experience. Instead of forty days, readers experience deep discipleship and renewal in a twenty-one day format. The uniqueness of both books is the inclusion of *all* areas necessary for full first love surrender to Jesus. It is the key missing element in many modern efforts at renewal. Full surrender by grace is the key to New Testament power for all believers!

To fully encounter God, I urge each reader to embrace this tool as a *relational journey* with Jesus, not just a book study. Remember God's glorious promise — *"if you seek Me with all your heart, you will find Me."* (Jeremiah 33:3, emphasis added) As we begin our journey, it is very important to stay focused on the awesome power of God's grace. Because of His grace in

Christ, God totally forgives and accepts His people! (Romans 4:5, 5:1; Ephesians 1:6)

Believers, *now* is the time to grow up in the specific commitments of seriously seeking the Lord. Today's typical patterns of prayer and surrender will not suffice for the things that lie ahead! If all we do is embrace another "temporary prayer emphasis," we will fail to see major change. It would be much akin to Jesus' analogy of "casting out a demon yet leaving the life clean and swept" (meaning vacant and unsurrendered to Christ.) *"The last state of that man is worse than the first."* (Matthew 12:45)

If all we do is embrace another emphasis yet return to the same inadequate levels of daily prayer, whatever renewal we might experience will not last. *However*, if we truly embrace a specific commitment to walk under Christ's Lordship, neither we nor the nation will ever be the same! Though it may seem impossible, let us continue to cry out for another great spiritual awakening. And even if it is too late for sweeping awakening of the whole nation, a great revival could surely come to your life and church. Be encouraged. If we take this journey seriously, we will never be the same. May we all embrace the covenant to a God-seeking life. Our great God deserves nothing less!

Towards the Next Great Awakening,

Twenty-One Days of Transformation
"Beginning Your Journey in Grace"

*A*s we begin this three week journey, it is vital to stay centered on God's grace. We embrace deeper cleansing and yielding as a love relationship, not as a legalistic attempt to somehow earn God's acceptance. Every step of our journey is by His grace and through His Spirit. If this experience is to greatly transform our hearts, we must keep our eyes squarely on Jesus, the Author and Finisher of our faith. Though we are *all* a "work in progress," God fully accepts us in Christ's righteousness. (Philippians 3:12; Hebrews 12:1) Our hope and confidence is in Him!

It is further important to remember *why* we embrace deeper cleansing and prayer. While we should certainly seek God's blessing and deliverance, these are not to be our primary motives. Our central motivation is to seek God's kingdom and spread His righteousness in all the earth. (Matthew 6:33) As God transforms **us** *"by the renewing of our minds,"* His glory will be spread in the entire world! (Romans 12:1-2) To more fully experience God in this journey, stay centered on five key points for victory.

Five Points for Victory

1. *Because we are "in Him," the indwelling Christ is our power for life and victory.* (Romans 6:6-14; Colossians 1:27) It is crucial to realize that victory **never** comes by legalism or self-effort. From beginning to end, victory comes by trusting Christ's life and victory in us! Only by faith can we believe Christ to live through us in the power of the Holy Spirit.[3] (Galatians 2:20, 3:1-3) No cleansing

journey is about "earning" God's acceptance. It is about embracing His grace in love and repentance.

2. *Do not be condemned or overwhelmed as God reveals many areas needing growth.* Remember that we are fully accepted and justified in Christ's blood and righteousness. (Romans 5:1, 8:1; Ephesians 1:6) Believers must keep their eyes on God's grace and not be defeated by condemnation. God cleanses and convicts to transform, not overwhelm His people with guilt. Through Christ, the Father accepts us through every step of our growth. Our journey to growth is a life-long process. As Christians we are not to coast or drift. (2 Corinthians 7:1; Philippians 3:12)

3. *Do not just confess sins — seriously work on forsaking them!* (Proverbs 28:13) God desires specific repentance, not general confession. We must remember that walking with God is not only about turning from sin, it is about embracing Christ's righteousness in the power of the Holy Spirit. True repentance is both a turning *from* sin and a turning *to* righteousness.[4] According to Scripture, we mostly overcome evil by embracing good. (Romans 12:21; Galatians 5:16) Embracing good requires specific steps of repentance and new obedience. As we embrace Christ's life by faith and choose righteousness, the power of the Holy Spirit replaces sin and self with more and more of Christ. In this study, we not only repent of sin, we *embrace* Christ's life and righteousness.

4. *Embrace ever-deepening holiness and yielding as a central part of your daily walk with Jesus.* Throughout Scripture, the Lord commands believers to have a burning daily *passion* for greater transformation in Christ's image. According to Jesus, a passion for growth and obedience is our primary expression of love for Him. Let this book be the beginning of continual growth in loving God. ***Do not view cleansing***

and prayer as a one-time emphasis that stops! In scores of New Testament passages, we are commanded to ever press onward in deeper surrender. (Matthew 5:6; Romans 12:1-2; 2 Corinthians 7:1; Philippians 2:12-13, etc.) Unfortunately, a major problem is the modern tendency to want to just "float along and be blessed." While we are wholly loved and accepted in Christ's grace the moment we are born again, we are *not* to just coast along. God's grace makes powerful ongoing growth both possible (and commanded) for all believers.

Many readers will continue to use the twenty-one day guide in their ongoing daily prayer times. By adding just a little time each day, believers can pray through all areas of life seven to ten times in a single year! With such Scripture-centered surrender, growth and transformation are phenomenal. (Romans 12:1-2; 2 Corinthians 3:18) Each time we pray through the cleansing Scriptures, God does a deeper work. One thing is certain — *none* of us outgrow the need for ongoing growth concerning the twenty-one Scripture topics in this book. Determine to use this Bible-filled tool as a template for ongoing growth.

5. *Trust God for the fullness and power of the Holy Spirit.* (Acts 1:8; Ephesians 5:18) To experience His fullness, simply *confess* all known sin, *surrender* to a new obedience and *believe* Him to fill you with His Spirit.[5] In Ephesians 5:18, we are commanded to be (being) filled by the Holy Spirit. Every day, simply ask for and receive this fullness by faith. And remember — God does not require perfect vessels, just hearts willing to be honest, surrendered and "pressing toward the mark." As you now begin your journey of surrender and prayer, do so with full confidence. When we "draw near to God, He draws near to us!" (James 4:8)

Week One

Knowing, Loving and Fearing God
"Returning to God in Lifestyle Worship"

*T*his first week of our journey is the most crucial of all! It establishes the foundational "motive and means" of all we are and do. In these first seven days, we focus on the very purpose of our existence. According to Scripture, *our whole life purpose is the passion to know, love and fear God in obedient lifestyle worship.* With God, it is all about our heart and passion for His glory and kingdom. (Isaiah 43:7; Ecclesiastes 12:13; Matthew 22:37; John 17:3; Colossians 3:17)

Believers, if our heart motive is not centered on loving, fearing and glorifying God, our efforts at cleansing will be self-seeking legalism. With God it is all about our grace-based, love relationship with Himself. *Nothing* in our walk with God should ever be about legalism or ritual. We embrace deeper yielding because we love Jesus and want to obey Him. (John 14:15)

As we begin this journey, every effort is total dependence upon God's grace and Spirit. We can do nothing apart from God's grace. Yet there is glorious news — we are *not* apart from God's grace! Indeed, we are fully accepted and counted righteous in Christ. (Romans 4:5; Ephesians 1:6)

To every believer, I say rejoice! As you embrace deeper yielding and prayer, God promises to revolutionize your life. (James 4:8-10) Rest assured, you can come boldly to His throne of grace. (Hebrews 4:16) God is more than willing to fill your heart with fervent love, reverential fear and deep heart knowledge of Himself.

Day One — Embracing First Love Passion for Jesus

"Lifestyle Worship is Our Primary Purpose"

Matthew 22:37 - *"You shall love the LORD your God with all your heart, with all your soul, and with all your mind.'"*

Matthew 6:33 - *"But seek first the kingdom of God and His righteousness, and all these things shall be added to you."*

Revelation 2:4, 3:15-16 - *"Nevertheless I have this against you, that you have left your first love...I know your works, that you are neither cold nor hot. I could wish you were cold or hot. So then, because you are lukewarm, and neither cold nor hot, I will vomit you out of My mouth.*

1 Corinthians 13:1-3 - *"Though I speak with the tongues of men and of angels, but have not love, I have become sounding brass, or a clanging cymbal. And though I have the gift of prophecy, and understand all mysteries and all knowledge; and though I have all faith, so that I could remove mountains, but have not love, I am nothing. And though I bestow all my goods to feed the poor, and though I give my body to be burned, and have not love, it profits me nothing."*

Above all else, our central life purpose is intense love and worship of God.[6] According to Scripture, our very reason for existence is to love, worship and glorify God. (Isaiah 43:7; Matthew 22:37; John 4:23) We are to *"Love the Lord our God with all our **heart**, soul, mind and strength."* (Matthew 22:37, emphasis added) Make no mistake — our level of worship flows directly from our level of love. Fervently loving and worshipping God involves three essential elements: (1) A burning personal passion for God and Christ, (2) reverential fear (or respect) of

God and hallowing His Name, (3) the commitment to know God in ever-deepening intimacy.

One of the greatest and wisest prayers in the Bible is Moses' prayer in Exodus 33:18, "*Lord, show me Your glory.*" Saints, we are to embrace a passion to ever-more fully know God's glory. The more we see God's glory, the more we will love and fear Him in daily worship. The more we see Him as He is, the more we will be on fire to spread His glory and kingdom. Virtually all sin stems from the failure to properly know, love and fear God. When our hearts are filled with fervent love and godly fear, everything else falls in place. Conversely, if we are filled with love of self and the world over God, spiritual motivation burns low and sin runs high.

The very reason we are created is to know, love and fear God in daily lifestyle worship!

A Love Above All Others

In Luke 14:26, Jesus says our love for Him is to be even stronger than love for parents, children and our own lives. In Revelation 2:1-4, Jesus commands us to have a burning "first love passion." Today, some erroneously think they are mainly identified by their vocation and that being a Christian is something of a side-line or Sunday thing. Such thinking is absolutely false. When we become a Christian, Jesus becomes our main identity and His mission our life purpose. *Everything* else is to be secondary.

At this juncture, I want to greatly encourage every reader. While such powerful love might sound impossible, God will surely provide the grace for glorious change. (Romans 5:5) If we sincerely ask and believe, the Holy Spirit will fill us with miraculous love for God and people.

Even to the most distracted weary believers, God can restore a burning love and passion. The key is to be honest and confess that our love has indeed become less than passionate. Be aware that any form of lukewarmness is utterly egregious to God! (Revelation 3:15-18) While in His grace, God forgives our lukewarmness, His grace also enables us to change.

Believers, we must never excuse or tolerate lukewarmness in our hearts. Since the Lord clearly commands us to repent and return to our first love, He surely gives the grace to do it. (Revelation 2:4, 3:15-19) Prayerfully (and honestly) pray through the following questions. Confess and forsake any hint of lukewarmness or lack of passion for spiritual growth and service. Place a check beside each area needing repentance and transformation.

Questions for Reflection: Was there a time you were more fervent in your passion for Christ and kingdom service? ___ Do my patterns of prayer, Bible study and service reveal first love passion or lukewarmness? ___ Does a frequent repeating of the same sins reveal a lack of passion to grow and obey God? ___ Have you allowed the busyness of life to dull your passion for spiritual growth, prayer and serving Jesus? ___ Does a lack of family prayer and Bible study reveal a lukewarm love and neglect of Christ's Lordship? ___ Have disappointments, problems or sufferings led to a "cooling off" toward God, prayer or service to others? ___

Is some of my spiritual motivation actually more from duty, guilt (or pay) than pure love and passion for Jesus? ___ Do I tend to think more about worldly issues than kingdom priorities? ___ Do I have "idols of the heart" such as work, family, sports or entertainment that often take precedence over God's word, prayer and service? ___ Am I actually more enthused and interested in hobbies, money, sports or work than spiritual growth and service for God? ___ Does the earthly focus of my thoughts indicate a lack of first love passion for Jesus? ___ Is there any sense in which I am spiritually cold or lukewarm? ___ By trusting God's grace, surrender your heart to a new passion for Christ and His kingdom.

Ask God for a spirit of deep brokenness over any hint of lukewarmness in your life. Surrender your heart and yield to Jesus. Claim God's glorious promise in 1 John 1:9. *"If we confess our sins, He is faithful and just to forgive us our sins and to cleanse us from all unrighteousness."* Remember, you are fully accepted and forgiven in Christ's righteousness! Believe Jesus to live through you by the Holy Spirit. (Romans 6:11) In the blanks below, identify your specific points for transformation.

_____

_____

_____

_____

_____

Now that you have yielded your heart to more passionately love Jesus, rejoice in God's full acceptance and forgiveness! (Ephesians 1:6; 1 John 1:9) Be determined to embrace the process of confession, repentance and growth as a daily lifestyle. By faith, claim the fullness and power of the Holy Spirit. (Luke 11:13) Spend time praying the following two prayers from your heart.

Day One Prayer Focus

📖 Thank God for His promised grace to live in first passion for Jesus. Trust Him to give you a heart on fire. Commit to prayer, Scripture, spiritual growth and service as your absolute top priorities. (Matthew 6:33, 22:37; Romans 12:1-2)

📖 Plead for God's mercy on the Church, nation and world. Pray that He would stay His righteous judgment and turn us to Himself in fervent love and deep repentance. (2 Chronicles 7:14; Psalm 85:4-7; Daniel 9:18-19; Hebrews 4:16; James 4:8-10; 1 Peter 4:17)

Day Two — Reverential Fear of God

"Hallowing His Name"

Leviticus 10:3 - *"And Moses said to Aaron, "This is what the LORD spoke, saying: 'By those who come near Me I must be regarded as holy; And before all the people I must be glorified.'"*

Ecclesiastes 12:13-14 - *"Let us hear the conclusion of the whole matter: Fear God and keep His commandments, For this is man's all. For God will bring every work into judgment, Including every secret thing, Whether good or evil."*

Proverbs 8:13 - *"The fear of the LORD is to hate evil; Pride and arrogance and the evil way And the perverse mouth I hate."*

Matthew 6:9 - *"In this manner, therefore, pray: Our Father in heaven, Hallowed be Your name."*

Isaiah 66:1-2 – *"Thus says the LORD: "Heaven is My throne, And earth is My footstool. Where is the house that you will build Me? And where is the place of My rest? For all those things My hand has made, And all those things exist," Says the LORD. "But on this one will I look: On him who is poor and of a contrite spirit, And who trembles at My word."*

2 Corinthians 7:1 - *"Therefore, having these promises, beloved, let us cleanse ourselves from all filthiness of the flesh and spirit, perfecting holiness in the fear of God."*

Second only to loving God is the command to *fear* Him in reverential awe and respect. (Ecclesiastes 12:13-14; 2 Corinthians 7:1) While fearing God does not mean a cringing dread of some cruel tyrant, it does mean a reverential respect for the One Who is utterly holy and deserves our full love, obedience and worship. Mark this well — God deserves all love, all worship, all reverence, all obedience, all trust, all surrender, all attention, all the time!

The biblical fear of God is the beginning of wisdom and keeps us from falling into sin. (Proverbs 1:7) Among the most troubling trends of our day is a wide-spread lack of reverential fear and awe of God. When believers do not hallow, respect and revere God as holy, lukewarmness and sin become rampant.

God deserves all love, all worship, all reverence, all obedience, all trust, all surrender, all attention, all the time!

The essence of fearing God is to continually recognize His awesome power, glory and holiness. In a day of shallow, unbalanced theology, it is crucial to realize God is *both* loving and holy. It is impossible to return to God if we do not acknowledge Him as He is. To approach Him, we are commanded to regard God as holy. (Leviticus 10:3) Never forget the constant refrain of God's awesome created beings around the throne — "*holy, holy, holy, Lord God Almighty.*" (Revelation 4:8(b)) Believers, this must be our cry as well.

As Lord of all, Jesus deserves nothing less than absolute surrender and fervent love. God is not some heavenly "Santa Claus" figure or "divine pal" we can shape and bend for our own desires. He is absolutely holy, sovereign God![7] As believers, we are "not our own and have been "bought with a price." (1 Corinthians 6:19-20) God is to be our absolute love and first priority. The following questions help us evaluate our level of godly reverence and respect for God's holiness. To experience deeper surrender and victory, prayerfully work through the reflective questions

Questions for Reflection — Is there a sense in which I take sin lightly by often repeating the same sins? ___ Have I neglected to fully revere God and tremble before His holy word? ___ Do I treat God more as a pal or Santa Claus figure than holy God and judge of all? ___ Do I frequently confess the same sins, but fail to become serious about turning from them? ___ This reveals a serious disrespect for the awesome cost it takes for God to forgive our sin. (That cost was Christ's suffering and death in our place.)

Do I treat God as if I can take or leave surrender of my whole life? ___ Have I failed to truly settle the Lordship issue by neglecting full surrender in certain areas of my life? ___ Do I often fail to "press toward the mark" and "perfect holiness in the fear of God?" ___ Is my personal pattern better described by drifting along than urgently pursuing and perfecting holiness? ___ Have I in any way spoken disrespectfully to or about God? ___ Does any of my speech, emails or texts reveal a lack of respect for God or others? ___ Do I act as if sin is no big deal because I am "under grace?" ___ (All such patterns reveal a lack of reverential fear and awe of God.)

Confess and forsake whatever God has revealed. Surrender your heart and yield to Jesus. Claim God's glorious promise in 1 John 1:9. *"If we confess our sins, He is faithful and just to forgive us our sins and to cleanse us from all unrighteousness."* You are fully accepted and forgiven in Christ's righteousness! Believe Jesus to live through you by the Holy Spirit. (Romans 6:11) In the blanks below, identify your specific points for transformation. _____

_____

_____

_____

Now that you have yielded your heart to more deeply reverence Jesus, rejoice in God's acceptance and forgiveness! (Ephesians 1:6; 1 John 1:9) Pause in prayer and ask Christ to empower you with the Holy Spirit. Be determined to embrace the process of confession, repentance and growth as a daily lifestyle. From your heart, lift the following prayers to God.

Day Two Prayer Focus

📖 Ask God to fill you with reverence and awe for His holy name. Confess any words or actions that do not revere God. Trust Him for a godly fear that is balanced with His grace. (Ecclesiastes 12:12-13; Matthew 6:9; 2 Corinthians 7:1)

📖 Cry out for deep brokenness, Godly fear and humble repentance to sweep God's people (Psalm 51:17; Proverbs 28:13; John 14:15; 2 Corinthians 7:1, 10; Ephesians 5:26-27; Hebrews 12:14)

Day Three — The Passion to More Fully Know and Seek God

Psalm 27:8 - *"When you said unto me seek my face, I said, your face O God I will seek."*

Psalm 42:1 - *"As the deer pants for the water brooks, So pants my soul for You, O God."*

Jeremiah 29:13 – *"And you will seek Me and find Me, when you search for Me with all your heart."*

John 17:3 - *"And this is eternal life, that they may know You, the only true God, and Jesus Christ whom You have sent."*

A most vital element of loving God is the commitment to continually seek to *know* Him in ever-deepening intimacy. If we truly love and fear God, we will spend attentive time in His word and prayer. Mark this well — a five minute quiet time on the run is *not* "seeking God with all our hearts." (Jeremiah 29:13) Such is not the pattern of Jesus, New Testament believers or great Christians throughout Church history. If we truly love someone and want to know them, we will give them *quality* time and *full* attention. That is both the nature and requirement of a love relationship.

Believers, we must never view Bible study as a duty or merely an intellectual pursuit. Abiding in prayer and Scripture is a love relationship of ever-seeking to more fully know God. When we truly know God, we have an insatiable desire to know Him even more. It is entirely disingenuous to say "we love God," yet consistently neglect quality time in His word and prayer. To love God is to seek Him and keep His commandments. (Psalm 27:8; John 14:15) But be encouraged. While five minutes on the run is not sufficient, neither does God require extensive time that is legalistic or out of reach. With God's grace, every believer can experience a life of ever-more fully knowing Jesus! By honest confession of our need to seek Him, we receive God's grace to experience hearts on fire for Christ.

Praying the Attributes and Names of God
The Prayer and Meditation that Transforms
(Romans 12:1-2; 1 Corinthians 3:18)

Among the most crucial ways to more deeply know God is to study His *names* and *attributes* in Scripture.[8] After all, if we really love someone, we want to ever-more deeply know their heart, nature and deepest thoughts. The more we meditate and pray through God's attributes and names, the more deeply we know, love and worship Him in Spirit and truth. In Malachi 3:16, God even promises very special blessing on those who *"fear the Lord and meditate on His name."* Yet sadly, many believers have never embraced even these most basic patterns of knowing God. In truth, most have never even been told they

The more we meditate and pray through God's attributes and names, the more deeply we know, love and worship Him in Spirit and truth.

should or taught how. (For a practical tool on praying God's attributes and names, contact my office. The tool is entitled, **My Covenant to Pray God's Attributes and Names**.)

As we continue this cleansing journey, I encourage every believer to remember God's incredible grace. Do not be overwhelmed or think first love and deeper knowledge are out of reach! Even as God convicts our hearts, His grace and power will transform us in His image. (Romans 12:1-2) Carefully pray through the following "Questions for Reflection." As God reveals points for repentance, simply confess your sin and trust His grace to help you change. God will begin a glorious transformation in your life!

Questions for Reflection: Have I rationalized that I am just an "average" Christian and therefore do not have to embrace deeper prayer and holiness? ___ Have I failed to hunger and thirst for deeper closeness with Jesus? ___ Have I been neglectful in daily prayer, Scripture study and closeness with Jesus? ___ Have I been content with little or no quiet time prayer and failed to hunger for greater spiritual power? ___

Do I show a lack of hunger and thirst for God by failing to consistently embrace ever-deeper surrender and cleansing? ___ Have I failed to frequently meditate and pray through God's attributes and names? ___ Does my failure to address damaged relationships reveal a low level of commitment to more fully know Christ? ___ (No one can be right with God if they neglect full forgiveness and reconciliation with others) Do I read only small sections of Scripture and spend mostly brief moments in prayer? ___

Am I more like a busy frantic Martha than a prayerful listening Mary? (Luke 10:38) Have I in any way viewed significant time in prayer and Scripture as a "duty" rather than a joyful personal love relationship with God? ___ Have I perhaps viewed this cleansing journey as a chore, rather than a glorious privilege to draw closer to Jesus? ___ Seeking closeness with Christ is to be our deepest joy. By trusting God's grace, surrender to a lifestyle of seeking to know Him in ever-deepening intimacy.

Claim God's glorious promise in 1 John 1:9. *"If we confess our sins, He is faithful and just to forgive us our sins and to cleanse us from all unrighteousness."* Dear reader, you are fully accepted and forgiven in Christ's righteousness! In the blanks below, identify your specific steps for knowing God in greater intimacy. _____

_____

_____

_____

Now that you have yielded your heart to more deeply know and seek Jesus, rejoice in God's acceptance and forgiveness! (Ephesians 1:6; 1 John 1:9) Pause in prayer and ask Christ to empower you with the Holy Spirit. From your heart, lift the following prayers to the throne of grace.

Day Three Prayer Focus

📖 Ask God for a passion to know Him more and more. Ask Him to show you His glory. Commit to spend quality time in Scripture, prayer and meditative listening. (Exodus 33:18; Psalm 27:8, 42:11; Jeremiah 29:13; John 17:3)

📖 Pray for an explosion of first love passion for Christ and a deep burden for lost humanity (Matthew 5:6, 44, 22:37-39; Philippians 2:13; 1 John 4:7-11, 20-21; Revelation 2:1-4, 3:15)

Day Four — Victory Over Insincere Worship

Worship as Our Lifestyle and Purpose

Psalm 29:2 – *"Give unto the LORD the glory due to His name; Worship the LORD in the beauty of holiness."*

Isaiah 43:7 – *"Everyone who is called by My name, Whom I have created for My glory; I have formed him, yes, I have made him."*

Amos 5:21-24 - *"I hate, I despise your feast days, and I do not savor your sacred assemblies. Though you offer Me burnt offerings and your gain offerings, I will not accept them."*

Matthew 15:8-9a - *"This people draw near to Me with their mouth, and honor Me with their lips: but their heart is far from Me. But in vain they do worship Me."*

John 4:23 - *"But the hour is coming, and now is, when the true worshippers will worship the Father in spirit and in truth: for the Father is seeking such to worship Him."*

Colossians 3:17 – *"And whatever you do in word or deed, do all in the name of the Lord Jesus, giving thanks to God the Father through Him."*

Believers, it is crucial to realize the very reason we are created is to continually *worship, love* and *glorify* God. These are our central purposes both now and forever! Our lives do not consist of money, comforts or things. (Luke 12:15) Knowing, loving and worshipping God is our all in all! It is indeed crucial to realize every aspect of our lives is to be worship, not just worship services. According to Jesus, lifestyle *obedience* is the primary expression of our love and worship. (John 14:15) For this reason, our "worship services" will never be deeper than our "worship walk" in daily life.

The above passages reveal God's strong displeasure with insincere worship and empty ritual. The very essence of worship is to bow before God in genuine loving reverence and obedient surrender. Yet, even many believers have forgotten the awesome holiness and majesty of our Creator. To many today, it is as if God exists mostly to fulfill all our desires and needs. We seriously compromise with sin yet still expect God to honor our prayers and receive our worship.

Worship is the Life We Live
(Not Just the Lyrics We Sing)

It seems many have forgotten that willful, habitual sin is equal to "trampling underfoot the precious blood of Jesus" (Hebrews 10:29). How can we sing *"You're All I Need"* or *"Brokenness is What I Long For,"* if we have little more than three minute prayer times or watch questionable movies? Singing nice lyrics does not automatically make them true in our lives. God is looking for *"truth in the inward parts."* (Psalm 51:6) He desires worship in Spirit and Truth (or sincerity).

It is further disturbing to see how thoughtlessly many receive the Lord's Supper. The Lord's Supper is a moment of supreme holiness and personal examination. In 1 Corinthians 11:28-30, Paul even states that sickness and death can result from irreverence for Christ's sacrifice. Yet many approach this holy moment of worship with absolutely no thought of confession or repentance.

The fact that God could bring judgment seems never to cross the minds of most modern saints.[9] Many have forgotten that *"judgment begins at the house of God."* (1 Peter 4:17) Most are oblivious to just how far we have moved from a biblical reverence and worship of holy God. But fear not — if we confess our need, God will fill us with genuine worship. Prayerfully work through the following questions.

Questions for Reflection: In coming to worship, is your primary purpose to bow before God in utter repentance and obedience? ____ Is your mind filled with godly fear and reverence for the

Lord? ___ Have you viewed worship more as a weekly one hour service than of a daily lifestyle of loving obedience? ___ (True worship is a lifestyle.) Do you really love and reverence God for Himself or mostly just seek His benefits? ___ Do you truly set aside Sunday for God or merely tip your hat for an hour before doing your own thing? ___

Have you taken the Lord's Supper without deep examination and personal repentance? ___ Do you frequently sing the worship hymns without deeply reflecting on the words? ___ Do you listen to sermons with little thought of immediate obedience to God's instructions? ___ Insincere, ritualistic worship is one of the most serious sins a believer can commit! Do you need to confess an inadequate reverence and worship of God? ___ Immediately confess this most serious of sins. Trust God to grant you the spirit of genuine reverence and worship. He will surely forgive and cleanse your heart! In the following spaces, list specific ways you can embrace deeper worship. _____

_____

_____

_____

As we confess our failures in the matter of worship, let us confidently claim the forgiveness and power of the covenant in Christ's blood. We are fully accepted and justified in Him! In your own words, embrace Christ's heart by praying the following prayers.

Day Four Prayer Focus

📖 Pray for God to enable you to worship Him in spirit, truth and beauty of holiness. Commit to surrender every area of your life to Christ's Lordship. Praise, obedience and loving surrender are the essence of true worship! (Psalm 29:2; John 4:23; Colossians 3:17)

📖 Cry out for a mighty movement of fervent personal and corporate prayer with spirit-led fasting (2 Chronicles 7:14; Joel 1:14, 2:12-18; Matthew 6:16-18, 17:21, 21:13; Mark 11:17; Acts 2:1, 4:30-31; James 5:16)

Day Five — Embracing Christ-Guided Thoughts

"Gaining Victory Over Lust, Impurity and Immorality"

Psalm 101:2-3 – *"I will behave wisely in a perfect way. Oh, when will You come to me? I will walk within my house with a perfect heart. I will set nothing wicked before my eyes; I hate the work of those who fall away; It shall not cling to me."*

Proverbs 23:7(a) – *"For as he thinks in his heart, so is he."*

2 Corinthians 10:5 - *"Casting down arguments and every high thing that exalts itself against the knowledge of God, bringing every thought into captivity to the obedience of Christ."*

Matthew 5:28 - *"But I say unto you, that whoever looks at a woman to lust for her has already committed adultery with her in his heart."*

Ephesians 5:5 - *"For this you know, that no fornicator, unclean person, nor covetous man, who is an idolater, has any inheritance in the kingdom of Christ and God."*

Over the last forty years, the world has witnessed an unprecedented explosion of immorality, perversion and pornography. Worst of all, this river of filth has spread far among believers and churches. The seeming anonymity of internet pornography has caused many to succumb to this moral and spiritual poison. Hardly a week goes by that we do not hear of marriages and ministries destroyed by pornography and wrong relationships.

Even when believers are not outwardly exposed, the inward spiritual damage is profound. Little grieves God's Sprit or blocks prayer like immoral viewing habits and resulting bondage to unclean imaginations. Mark this well — Jesus cannot be Lord of any life if He is not Lord of one's eyes. Sadly, many have become so spiritually desensitized to impurity; they are unaware of the degree to which God's Spirit is currently grieved and quenched. As you read the following reflective questions, ask God to open your eyes to any compromise with lust or immorality.

Questions for Reflection: Carefully and honestly reflect on the type of thoughts that occupy your mind. Is your mind filled more with thoughts of Christ or consumed with earthly issues? ___ Do you often think far more about work or recreation than spiritual growth and serving Christ? ___ Does anxiety and fear have a grip on your mind? ___ Are you plagued with fearful or angry thoughts? ___

Do you watch programs, movies or websites that stimulate improper thoughts and feelings? ___ Are you frequently conscious of unclean thoughts or motives? ___ Do you often have thoughts you would be ashamed for others to know? ___

Do you have wandering eyes? ___ Have you committed any form of sexual immorality, uncleanness or perversion? ___ Are you watching anything you would be uncomfortable for your spouse, parents, pastor or children to see you watch? ___ Do you make excuses by saying "There's nothing else to watch"? ___

Are you dressing in ways designed to incite lust in the opposite sex? ___ Are you in the habit of reading things that are suggestive or unclean? ___ Do you watch today's talk shows that regularly joke about immorality and perversion? ___ Do you fund Hollywood's poison by going to questionable movies or purchasing videos? ___

If you sense God's conviction, be specific in your confession. Decide how you are going to change your thoughts to remove the patterns of sin. Be specific about the thoughts you need to change. It is vital that you replace unclean thoughts with other thoughts that focus on Christ. Memorizing key Scriptures will provide a powerful tool for removing inappropriate thoughts. Every time an unclean thought arises, you can replace it with Scripture and a prayerful focus on God. If you follow this process, God will transform your mind! (Romans 12:2)

Write down any sinful thought pattern God brings to your attention. For each one, ask God's forgiveness and trust Him to renew your mind (Romans 12:2). Resolve to take every thought captive to the Lordship of Christ. What changes would help you guard and transform your thoughts? List them here.

_____

_____

_____

_____

Day Five Prayer Focus

📖 Ask God to help you take every thought captive to the obedience of Jesus Christ. Confess and forsake any angry, fearful or lustful thoughts. Trust Jesus to help you "put off" sin and "put on" His righteousness. (Psalm 101:2-3; Proverbs 23:7a; Matthew 5:28; 2 Corinthians 10:5)

📖 Plead for God's powerful manifest presence, a restraining of evil and a mighty outpouring of His Spirit (Exodus 33:15; 1 Kings 8:11; Isaiah 59:19; Zechariah 4:6; Acts 1:8, 2:1-2, 4:31)

Day Six — Embracing Brokenness and Humility

"Victory Over Pride and Prejudice"

Psalm 51:17 - *"The sacrifices of God are a broken spirit, These 0 God, You will not despise."*

Philippians 2:3-4 - *"Let nothing be done through selfish ambition or conceit, but in lowliness of mind let each esteem others better than himself. Let each of you look out not only for his own interests, but also for the interests of others."*

James 2:1, 4 — *"My brethren, do not hold the faith of our Lord Jesus Christ, the Lord of glory, with partiality.......have you not shown partial among yourselves, and become judges of evil thoughts?"*

1 Peter 5:5 - *"God resists the proud, But gives grace to the humble."*

1 John 2:16 – *"For all that is in the world--the lust of the flesh, the lust of the eyes, and the pride of life--is not of the Father but is of the world."*

In many ways, pride and self-will are the roots of all sin and rebellion against God. Especially today, pride is the underlying foundational sin so easily overlooked. It has innumerable forms. The most common patterns of pride generally center in four forms.

One such form is the strong desire to impress people through appearance, money, status symbols or accomplishments. Even the slightest desire to exalt and glorify ourselves is highly offensive to God's Spirit. A *second* form is any hint of self-righteousness or over-assessment of our spirituality and power. A *third* form is a tendency to spiritually coast and abandon the hunger and thirsting after greater holiness. Still a *fourth* form of pride is to assess my life or church as more empowered or spiritual than its true condition. God says we are not to "measure ourselves by ourselves" or to view ourselves as "rich and in need of nothing" when by His standards we are actually lukewarm and weak. (2 Corinthians 10:12; Revelation 3:18) Pride is a subtle sin so easily overlooked.

Perhaps the worst form of pride is the attitude of spiritual complacency that sees little need for ongoing cleansing and growth in one's own life. If the apostle Paul needed to "press toward the mark," how much more do we? The Greek word for "press" (*diōkō*) has the rich meaning of to *pursue* or follow, to urgently press forward.[10] True revival always begins with deep humility and brokenness over sin (2 Chronicles 7:14). As believers, we are to ever be "pressing toward the mark and perfecting holiness in the fear of God." (2 Corinthians 7:1; Philippians 3:12-14) Being "under grace" in no way means we can just leisurely *coast* in the Christian life.

Questions for Reflection: Do you think yourself quite spiritual? ___ Do you often criticize and judge others? ___ Do you spend daily time allowing God to deeply search your life or do you feel you need little cleansing? ___ Are you truly broken and contrite over your shortcomings or do you tend to think, "Oh well, no one is perfect?" ___

Are you desperately hungry to see a mighty move of God or are you somewhat complacent? ___ Do you come across as having a "holier than thou attitude?" ___ If you feel that you have nearly "arrived" and need little growth, you are guilty of the worst form of spiritual pride. God hates self righteousness and spiritual complacency.

Do you have a significant tendency to become angry when others do not notice and praise you? ___ Is there any desire to impress people by your appearance, money or accomplishments? ___ Do you in any way fail to put all the focus on God's grace by drawing attention to yourself? ___

Do you tend to look down on people who are not as financially affluent? ___ Conversely, do you resent those who have more monetarily? ___ Do you closely associate only with your own race or culture? ___ Are you suspicious of those from a different race, culture or background? ___ Do you think you are too good to closely associate with someone you consider unattractive or not part of the "in crowd?" ___ Conversely, do you tend to resent people more physically attractive or gifted than yourself? ___ Have you sought to reach out to other culture groups or have you settled into a social "comfort zone?" ___

Immediately confess and forsake all sins of pride or prejudice. Believe Christ for a spirit of genuine humility and contriteness of heart. List specific ways you can embrace greater brokenness and humility. _____

_____

_____

_____

Rest in the all-sufficient grace of God. In Jesus' name, lift the following prayers to God. Ask for His fullness and power.

Day Six Prayer Focus

📖 Confess and forsake any patterns of self-exaltation or condescension toward others. Ask God's grace for a genuine heart of brokenness and humility. Trust God for brokenness, humility and contriteness of heart. (Psalm 51:17; Philippians 2:3-4; James 2:1,4, 4:10; 1 Peter 5:5; 1 John 2:16)

📖 Pray for a burning passion for evangelism, discipleship and missions to sweep God's people (Matthew 24:14, 28:18-20; Luke 19:10; Acts 1:8; Romans 9:1-3)

Day Seven — Victory Over Fear and Unbelief

"Embracing the Courage to Stand for Truth"

Joshua 1:9- *"Have I not commanded you? Be strong and of good courage; do not be afraid, nor be dismayed, for the LORD your God is with you wherever you go."*

Mark 8:38 – *"For whoever is ashamed of Me and My words in this adulterous and sinful generation, of him the Son of Man also will be ashamed when He comes in the glory of His Father with the holy angels."*

Mark 9:23 – *"Jesus said unto him, If you can believe, all things are possible to him who believes."*

Philippians 4:6 – *"Be anxious for nothing; but in everything by prayer and supplication with thanksgiving, let your requests be made known unto God."*

Hebrews 11:6 - *"But without faith it is impossible to please Him: for he that cometh to God must believe that He is, and that He is a rewarder of those who diligently seek Him."*

Unbelief is one of the most damaging sins a believer can commit. It was mostly unbelief that caused the children of Israel to die in the wilderness.[11] Unbelief seriously short-circuits God's power in the believer's life. Because of unbelief, many believers live in weakness and defeat. Through lack of faith, crucial prayers go unanswered. (Matthew 13:58) In many believers, this condition is often subtle and unconscious. Over time, it becomes so ingrained there is a continual mindset of doubt and low expectation.

In the gospels, Jesus repeatedly emphasized the importance of expectant faith. It shall be unto you "according to your faith" is among Jesus' most preeminent statements. While it is certainly possible to move into an excessive "name it and claim it" type emphasis, most believers are settling for much too little.

The Importance of Standing Bold for Jesus
(Mark 8:38)

Today, a common element of unbelief is the tendency to become intimated before a godless, hostile society. In our increasingly immoral society, both churches and individuals face growing pressure to compromise with evil. (And sadly, far too many are giving in.) To be "politically correct," many churches and Christians have already condoned lifestyles the Bible emphatically calls evil. Many churches ignore key Scripture and teachings because it wouldn't be "popular." According to Mark 8:38, this is a direct *betrayal* and *denial* of Christ!

Especially in coming days, believers will be put to severe tests by an ever more perverse society. Yet, this very testing may actually be among the best things that could happen to us! We should never pray for revival just so we can avoid suffering. It may well take greater sufferings to bring full revival. We must not give in to any form of fear or timidity in the coming trials of the hour.

Questions for Reflection: Are you frequently filled with more doubt than faith? ___ Do you tend to worry and fret rather than trust God? ___Are you fully resting in God's promises or are you frequently anxious? ___ Have you excused the sin of unbelief by claiming to be a "born worrier?" ___ Do you excuse your doubt by saying, "I have good reason to worry?" ___ Have you let disappointments weaken your faith and prayer life? ___ A pattern of worry is not just a weakness; it is a willful sin against God. God promises perfect peace to those who choose to trust rather than fear. (Isaiah 26:3) Do you need to confess the sin of unbelief and worry? ___ (You may also need to talk to a godly counselor or doctor about the roots of your anxiety.)

Are you prepared to stand for God's truth no matter what the cost? ___ Do you rationalize and make excuses for rejecting biblical standards? ___ When the pressure is on, do you ignore Scripture and go with the crowd? ___ If God convicts you of compromise, please don't make further excuses. Fully confess the sin and believe God for supernatural power to stand strong. There is incredible reward for all who are persecuted for righteousness sake! (Matthew 5:12) Remember, you can never lose when you stand for Christ and you can never win when you go with the godless crowd. Best of all, you can trust God for the grace to stand! From your heart, lift these prayers to the Father.

Friend, no matter how long you have had doubt or timidity, God can give you boldness, faith and a supernatural peace. Don't settle for anything less! List your specific fears that need to be released and renounced. _____

_____

_____

_____

_____

God is faithful and worthy of your full trust. Rest in His grace and pray the following prayers.

Day Seven Prayer Focus

☐ Confess and forsake doubt, fear or timidity. Ask God to fill you with great boldness and mountain-moving faith. Covenant to trust God fully and stand boldly for Christ no matter the cost. (Mark 8:38, 11:22-24; Hebrews 11:6)

☐ Plead for church leaders filled with holy boldness, fervent prayer, spiritual power and strong scripture focus (1 Corinthians 2:4; 1 Timothy 3:1-2; 2 Timothy 1:6-7)

Week Two

Embracing Godly Attitudes and Right Relationships

*T*he second week involves the foundational areas of godly attitudes and right relationships. Second only to heart passion and purity are our *attitudes* and *relationships*. Attitudes, thoughts and relationships are the very essence of our lives and character. (Proverbs 23:7) Because God created us as both rational and relational beings, the enemy is always seeking to gain strongholds in our thoughts and relationships.

As God evaluates our lives, He not only views our outward actions, but especially the attitudes and thoughts behind them. (Psalm 19:14) Indeed, many times "how" someone says something carries almost as much weight as "what" they actually say. Attitudes are central to relationships. God is deeply focused on the meditations of our hearts. Inner attitudes dictate our outward actions and relationships. Ask God to open your eyes to any heart attitudes that need to change. And be encouraged — God is more than willing to transform our thoughts and relationships with others. (Romans 12:1-2; 1 Corinthians 2:16)

Day Eight — Victory Over Anger and Division

"Embracing a Kind, Gentle Spirit"

John 13:34-35 – "*A new commandment I give to you, that you love one another; as I have loved you, that you also love one another. By this all will know that you are My disciples, if you have love for one another.*"

1 Corinthians 1:10 – *"Now I plead with you, brethren, by the name of our Lord Jesus Christ, that you all speak the same thing, and that there be no divisions among you, but that you be perfectly joined together in the same mind and in the same judgment."*

Ephesians 4:29-32 - *"Let no corrupt word proceed out of your mouth, but what is good for necessary edification, that it may impart grace to the hearers. And do not grieve the Holy Spirit of God, by whom you were sealed for the day of redemption. Let all bitterness, wrath, anger, clamor, and evil speaking be put away from you, with all malice. And be kind to one another, tenderhearted, forgiving one another, even as God in Christ forgave you."*

1 Timothy 5:17 – *"Let the elders who rule well be counted worthy of double honor, especially those who labor in the word and doctrine."*

The primary mark of a Spirit-filled believer is a kind, loving spirit. Conversely, a primary mark of a carnal believer (or lost church member) is a critical, angry attitude.[12] A sure indicator of carnality is a loud, pushy attitude which demands its own way. A high temper is a calling card of an unsurrendered heart. Speech (or cyber activity) that is divisive and rancorous reveals the opposite of a Spirit-guided mind. Little brings more shame to God or hindrance to the Holy Spirit. (John 13:34-35)

A forgiving attitude is a primary mark of someone right with God. Yet sadly, it is all too common for people to be highly religious, yet judgmental and unloving. Pharisees come in many shapes and varieties. Through lack of love and unforgiveness, family members often build relationship barriers in their homes. Though we may "say" we forgive, we really don't. If we frequently rehearse angry words we would like to say to someone, we have definitely *not* forgiven them "from the heart." (Matthew 18:35; Mark 11:25)

While it is certainly not wrong to feel pain when we are hurt, it is wrong to hold onto bitterness. Being loving and forgiving does not mean we have to feel rosy about all people and situations. Do not condemn yourself if you still have some battles with your feelings. The full healing of your emotions may well be a process. Yet by God's grace, we can learn to love with Christ's unconditional love. Love means we "choose" to be kind and forgiving in spite of feelings to the contrary. By God's grace, inner healing will surely come. Yet to embrace repentance, we must choose to forgive and release the bitterness. Until we fully release anger and bitterness, disunity and fighting remain preeminent.

The Critical Importance of Church Unity
(John 13:34, 17:21; 1 Corinthians 1:10)

Virtually nothing dishonors Christ or pleases Satan more than bickering among God's people. Yet tragically, church bickering and division are epidemic. Today's generation has also witnessed a shocking increase of preachers and lay leaders being fired or mistreated for relatively small, (often exaggerated) reasons. Certainly when a leader sins, he or she must be dealt with. Yet today, many churches have forgotten the vital biblical principle of respect and honor for those who lead the church. In many churches, the Holy Spirit is quenched because the congregation has sinned against a pastor or church leader.

Before churches can experience full revival, they often must seek forgiveness from pastors or leaders they have mistreated. Many churches may also need to ask forgiveness from a former pastor or lay leader. (In other cases, pastors must ask the forgiveness of churches they have wronged.) At least among some, there is an encouraging trend of churches and pastors reconciling over past problems. The result is a mighty release of God's manifest presence!

Questions for Reflection: Do you have a kind, gentle spirit or are you more argumentative, loud and contentious? ___ Are you often insensitive to the feelings and needs of others? ___ Do you tend to look for reasons to pick people apart? ___ Are you quick to get angry and speak your mind? ___ Do you blog, email, tweet or forward things you would not likely say to someone's face? ___ Do you make excuses by saying, "I can't help it, that's just my personality?" ___ Are you known as a peacemaker who strengthens church unity or, are you often part of some contentious argument? ___ Do others characterize you as having a gentle and quiet spirit? ___

Do you email, forward or text things that are in any way exaggerated, inaccurate or unkind? ___ Do you increase the faith of your church by a positive attitude or, do you tear it down by focusing on its imperfections? ___ Are you quick to divide up and "take sides?" ___ Are you known as a complainer and one who is easily upset? ___ Have you been harshly critical and condemning of those with different tastes in music and worship style? As people read this section, do you think others may be thinking about you and your patterns? ___ (If so, there is an immediate need for deep humble repentance, *not* defensiveness.)

Be completely honest in evaluation of your heart attitude. Ask for God's forgiveness and cleansing. Be specific about ways to change your attitude (especially with family). List them here.

_____

_____

_____

_____

Be confident in God's forgiveness and grace. Take a moment to meditate on the prayers below. With a heart of faith, lift the following requests to God.

Day Eight Prayer Focus

📖 Confess and forsake any patterns of angry bickering, gossip, disrespect or division. Ask forgiveness of all you have offended and forgive all who have offended you. Trust for God to fill you with loving kindness, respect for leaders and a spirit of biblical unity. (John 13:34; 1 Corinthians 1:10; Ephesians 4:27-32)

📖 Cry out for supernatural love and unity to sweep churches, denominations and families (John 13:34-35, 15:12, 17:20-22; Acts 2:1, 42-47; 1 Corinthians 1:10; Ephesians 4:29-32)

Day Nine — Overcoming Greed and Worldliness

1 Timothy 6:6, 8-10 - *"Now godliness with contentment is great gain...And having food and clothing, with these we shall be content. But those who desire to be rich fall into temptation and a snare, and into many foolish and harmful lusts which drown men in destruction and perdition. For the love of money is a root of all kinds of evil, for which some have strayed from the faith in their greediness, and pierced themselves through with many sorrows."*

1 John 2:15-17 - *"Do not love the world or the things in the world. If anyone loves the world, the love of the Father is not in him. For all that is in the world—the lust of the flesh, the lust of*

the eyes, and the pride of life—is not of the Father but is of the world."

Covetousness, materialism and worldliness are among the most pervasive (yet unacknowledged) sins of modern Christians.[13] Quite often, believers are blind to the materialism that subtly saturates our very souls. Rather than adhering to God's standard of moderation, high debt has become the norm.

Many believers seriously covet the symbols of worldly status and wealth. Our very affluence has become a huge spiritual hindrance. In today's churches, many have moved far from Paul's simple command, *"Be content with such things as you have."* (Hebrews 13:5)

Questions for Reflection: Anything we put ahead of God is an idol. Do you manage to find money for most everything else *except* tithes and offerings to God's kingdom? ___ Do you barely tithe and yet pay high interest to creditors? ___ In purchases, have you been motivated more by greed than seeking God's direction? ___ Does your financial history reflect biblical principles of low debt and modest living? ___

Has your debt caused you to miss payments and thus damage your witness? ___ Do you lust for things? ___ Would you be willing to live with less in order to embrace more God-centered patterns for your money? ___ Financial pressures strain many marriages. Is high debt straining yours? ___ Do you spend so much on non-essentials you are prevented from giving generously to hurting people and missions? ___ Do you carefully calculate a tithe then barely give beyond it? ___ (True grace giving is *well above* a tithe.)

Can you confidently (and sincerely) say "Jesus Christ is in full control of my desires and finances?" ___ Have you fervently prayed about financial decisions or simply flowed with the materialism of the world? ___ Today there are excellent books and resources to help you reduce debt and break the bondage to covetousness.

Please do not ignore God's conviction in this crucial area of life! Be specific about the changes God wants you to embrace. Take a moment and decide on your first steps of repentance. Write them here. _____

_____

_____

Day Nine Prayer Focus

 📖 Confess and forsake any patterns of greed, materialism or worldliness. Trust Jesus for eternal values and love of God. (1 Timothy 6:6, 8:10; 1 John 2:15-17)

 📖 Pray for powerful faith, pure motives and godly wisdom in seasons of judgment (Joshua 1:9; Jeremiah 29:16-18, 45:5; Acts 4:29-31; Matthew 6:33, 9:29, 16:18, 17:20; Mark 9:23, 11:22-24; 2 Timothy 1:7; James 4:1-4)

Day Ten — Overcoming Unclean Speech and Inappropriate Patterns Online

Matthew 12:36 – *"But I say to you that for every idle word men may speak, they will give account of it in the day of judgment."*

Ephesians 4:29(a) - *"Let no corrupt word proceed out of your mouth."*

Ephesians 5:4 - *"neither filthiness, nor foolish talking, nor coarse jesting, which are not fitting, but rather giving of thanks."*

James 1:19 – *"So then, my beloved brethren, let every man be swift to hear, slow to speak, slow to wrath."*

God places enormous importance on our speech. In Matthew 12:36, Jesus makes a sobering statement. *"But I say unto you that for every idle word men may speak, they will give account of it in the day of judgment."* Today's society has experienced an unprecedented explosion of vile and wicked speech.[14]

A similar statement of relevance is from James 1:26. *"If anyone among you thinks he is religious, and does not bridle his tongue but deceives his own heart, this one's religion is useless."* Beyond question, bridled tongues (and Internet) are crucial to Christ's reign in our lives! The Greek word for "bridle" (*chalinagōgeō*) means to *curb*.[15] No one can be right with God if they are not Spirit-guided and controlled in all speech, email or texting. (James 1:26)

Sadly, the Internet has taken anger, division and slander to levels never imagined. Far too often, believers email or forward things online they would never say in person. Many seem to forget that every Bible command for godly speech applies as much (or more) to the Internet!

Often without even knowing it, many believers have become "desensitized" to significant sins of speech. They are routinely reading, saying or forwarding things they would not have done just five years previous. Yet of course, God's standard has not moved one inch. Ask God for discernment as you prayerfully examine your words and social media patterns.

Questions for Reflection: Do you ever speak slang words that are crude and inappropriate? ___ Do you use God's name in any way other than worship, honor and praise? ___ Have you engaged in off color jokes or conversation? ___ Has the filthiness of our society crept into your speech? ___ Do you use any slang to add emphasis to what you're saying? ___ In Matthew 5:37, Jesus strongly condemned the use of slang or slanderous speech.

For some, the Internet has become gossip and slander on steroids. Many are blogging, tweeting or forwarding things that are angry, untrue and/or unbalanced. Even when what is being said may be true, an indiscriminant global forum is *no* place to be blasting it to all the earth.

Have you blogged, tweeted or forwarded anything that contradicts clear biblical principles for godly communications, actions and kind attitude? ___ Do you sense people reading these questions will think of you? ___ If so, there is need for deep, honest examination. Mark this well — we are many times more accountable for what we say online because it goes many times farther and cannot be retrieved! Honestly examine your speech and Internet use. Ask God for His forgiveness. Be specific in your confession of improper speech. Fully surrender your speech to the Lordship of Jesus Christ. List key areas that need adjustments. _____

_____

_____

_____

As we confess and forsake impure speech, we can place our full trust in Jesus, the *"author and finisher of our faith."* (Hebrews 12:2) From your heart, lift the following prayers to God.

Day Ten Prayer Focus

📖 Confess and forsake any communication patterns that are excessive, unbalanced or unkind. Pray for total surrender of every word spoken, texted, tweeted or emailed. Trust Jesus to be your power and wisdom for attitudes, words and cyberspace fully yielded to the Holy Spirit. (Matthew 12:36; Ephesians 4:29-32a; Ephesians 5:4; James 3:1-4)

📖 Plead for churches to fully proclaim Christ's preeminence, Calvary's cross and true new-birth conversion (John 3:3, 13:32, 16:8-14; Acts 4:12; Romans 6:1-14; Philippians 2:5-11; Colossians 1:9-18)

Victory Over Wrong Relationships

*I*n today's society, there is nothing more urgent than a move of God in restored relationships. From broken families to split churches, we are a people inundated with unaddressed bitterness and disunity. Today, a true return to God requires a *flood* of forgiveness and reconciliation. For most modern believers, the most common place we lose God's fullness is in our relationships.

Relationship sins generally fall in five major areas. In each area, we must be willing to take specific actions of repentance. While God is ready and able to forgive and transform, we must be willing to humbly repent. But let every believer be encouraged. By God's abundant grace, we *can* repent. Relationships can be healed and we can change! Pray through the following pages with a listening heart.

Day Eleven — Embracing Biblical Reconciliation

An Absolute Spiritual Necessity

With God, everything is about relationship! He said the very essence of all commandments is loving God and one another in Christ's power. (Matthew 22:37-39; Colossians 1:27) For this reason, it is essential to be fully honest about people you have hurt or offended either now or in the past. It is so very easy to overlook and minimize our own faults.

In Matthew 5:23-24, Jesus was emphatic about the importance of getting right with those you have offended. *"Therefore, if you bring your gift to the altar, and there remember that your brother has something against you, leave your gift before the altar, and go your way. First be reconciled to your brother, and then come and offer your gift."*

According to Christ, "Your relationship with God is greatly hindered until you humble yourself and seek reconciliation with all you have offended!" In essence Jesus was saying "Do not come to My altar if you will not seek forgiveness of those you have offended." Dear readers, I am not suggesting this is easy, but Jesus clearly states it is absolutely *necessary*. Countless Christians lack power because they have ignored this foundational command.

Take the next several moments to carefully consider those you may have offended. *Please* resist the common tendency to rush or gloss over this issue. When God reveals people you have hurt or slighted, resolve to go to them and ask their forgiveness. Yet, do not go and try to defend yourself or get the battle started again. Just go in simple humility and love. Furthermore, do not think you have failed if they refuse to forgive you. Your responsibility is to do your part in a humble and loving manner. How they respond is their responsibility.

Tremendous miracles occur in families when someone is willing to humbly ask forgiveness for a wrong. Very often, it starts with one person taking the first step. Powerful church wide revivals have often hinged on one or two church members getting truly right with one another. When just one or two persons humble themselves and ask forgiveness, it may well help many others take the same step. It is almost like "the (spiritual) dam breaks" and floods of revival may soon sweep many others. This principle is equally true in families.

Believers, we must understand that so called "little" rifts between Christians can quench God's Spirit for a whole church or family! In God's eyes, rifts are more than little. Each believer must remember a vital truth — the Holy Spirit is very sensitive and relationships are central. Are you waiting on someone else in your church to make the first move? How about your family? Have you reasoned that others are more guilty than you so they should act first? *Stop* such reasoning! Do what you know is right regardless of others' response.

Questions for Reflection: Is there anyone in your family you have offended, yet failed to ask forgiveness? ___ How about in your present church family (or churches from the past?) ___ Are any faces coming to mind right now? ___ (If so, you likely know exactly who they are.) Have you avoided giving serious consideration as to whether there are persons with whom you need to reconcile? ___ Deep down, do you sense God is telling you to openly ask for forgiveness? ___ If so, you could well be a huge key to whether or not God moves in your church and/or family.

Please do not deny or marginalize your need to go to *any* and *all* you have offended! If you think of people you even *might* have offended, there is a good chance you have. Do not delay or talk yourself out of obedience. *Do not* wait on others to take the first step! Above all, do not let pride stop your obedience. Be very specific and do not rush or gloss over these vital issues. List anyone to whom you sense a need to go and ask forgiveness.

_____

_____

_____

As believers, we are fully forgiven and empowered by the covenant of Christ's blood and indwelling life. When we plead His precious blood and wholly trust in His grace, victory is surely ours! From your heart, pray the following prayers.

Day Eleven Prayer Focus

📖 Ask God for the honesty to fully embrace the command for reconciliation. Confess and forsake any pride or stubbornness that prevents your asking forgivingness of others. Trust Jesus to be your strength and wisdom to obey. (Matthew 5:23-24; Hebrews 12:14)

📖 Cry out for an explosion of sound biblical doctrine and theology with full exaltation of God's glory and grace (1 Chronicles 29:10-13; Isaiah 42:8; Acts 20:27; 1 Corinthians 1:29; Ephesians 1:3-6, 2:7-9; 1 Timothy 1:17)

Day Twelve — Releasing All Unforgiveness
The Essential Key to Victory

In Matthew 6:14-15, Jesus made a statement of phenomenal importance. *"For if you forgive men their trespasses, your heavenly Father will also forgive you. But if you do not forgive men their trespasses, neither will your Father forgive your trespasses.*" In Matthew 18:35, the Lord even said, "*you must forgive from the heart*." (emphasis added) Obviously, Jesus is well aware of our tendency to "say" we have forgiven yet still hold onto grudges in our hearts.

According to Scripture, many prayers get no higher than the ceiling because we are holding inner resentment and bitterness against other persons. (Psalm 66:18; Mark 11:25) Jesus says we must not only forgive people, we must forgive them "from the heart." Matthew 18:35, "*So My heavenly Father also will do to you, if each of you, from his heart, does not forgive his brother his trespasses.*" (emphasis added) Today, it is incredibly common for people to "say" they have forgiven someone when in their heart, they really haven't.

Many people hold overt or secret bitterness against friends or family members. In other cases, it may be toward strangers who have wronged them. Especially today, believers need to be aware that we can develop bitterness toward politicians, social activists, and entertainers who attack godly values. While we must always stand strong for truth, we must not harbor hatred against those who attack us. We must never cease to hate sin, but we must always love the sinner. Ask God to search your heart and reveal any patterns of bitterness or unforgiveness.

It is even possible to hold secret bitterness against God. Some people privately resent the fact that God allowed some personal tragedy or didn't answer an urgent prayer. Others harbor bitterness because God blesses others in ways He has not blessed them. Far too many Christians have cooled off in their service and worship because they are hurt or disappointed. This is a strong indication of harboring resentments. But be encouraged — God's grace is sufficient for change!

Questions for Reflection: Is there anyone or any situation about which you harbor the slightest bitterness or resentment? ____ Do you frequently brood over things someone (or group) has done or is doing to wrong you? ____ Do you often rehearse angry things you would like to say or do? ____ Have you made an excuse by saying, "I just cannot forgive certain people?" ____ (Yet God says we can do all things through Christ and that His grace is sufficient.) Have you secretly resented God for allowing some painful situations in your life? ____ Have you "cooled off" toward God because He disappointed you in some manner? ____ Be honest with yourself and fully confess these sins. Make a definite decision to harbor no bitterness against anyone. And remember, forgiveness is a choice, not a feeling. Yet if you choose to forgive, God will increasingly change your feelings. List people and situations you need to forgive.

_____

_____

_____

_____

As we confess our sins of unforgiveness and subsequent bitterness, Christ's indwelling power is sufficient to give us victory (Colossians 1:27). Since He has so richly forgiven us, we can surely forgive others by His grace. Ask God for the fullness and power of the Holy Spirit. Fervently lift the following petitions to the throne of grace.

Day Twelve Prayer Focus

📖 Ask God to fill you with His own grace and love for those who have wronged you. Confess and forsake any angry thoughts or actions toward others. Yield all bitterness and resentment. Covenant to forgive others as Christ has forgiven you. Commit to pray and do good for enemies. (Mark 11:25; Luke 6:35; Ephesians 4:31-32)

📖 Plead for God to rend the heavens in sweeping revival and to transform the nations in spiritual awakening. cry out for Christ's swift return! (Psalm 2:8, 72:11, 85:6-7; Isaiah 64:1; Acts 2:1-2, 4:30-31; Ephesians 5:26-27; Revelations 22:17, 20)

Day Thirteen — Surrendering Improper Relationships

"Have No Appearance of Evil"

An improper relationship can be anything from adultery and fornication to simply being inappropriately close to someone. Improper relationships involve many things besides physical immorality. Because it is so easy to rationalize, this sin has become epidemic among Christians. It is the very soil from which adultery and fornication typically grow.

Facebook and other media have exploded these trends exponentially. Shocking numbers are spending so much time online, they are neglecting personal relationships in their own homes. Or even worse, they are communicating with certain people online far more than is appropriate. (In so many cases, a certain "friend" on social media has definitely become more than a friend.) Either the amount or nature of certain communications have definitely gone too far.

Ask God to reveal any relationships that are improper or out of balance. It is vital that you stop it now before it gets worse. Be honest with God and with yourself. And, do not despair; God will give you the strength to change! Prayerfully consider the following questions.

Questions for Reflection: A young person may be emotionally involved with someone too old or vice versa. Is this true of any of your relationships? ___ A husband may be too emotionally close to a female friend or work mate. A wife may be too emotionally involved with a male friend or work mate. Has workplace or Facebook sharing gotten out of hand? ___

Husbands and wives may be sharing things with others that should only be shared with their mate. Spouses may spend too much time with friends and/or co-workers to the neglect of their marriage partner. Parents can be too involved in the lives of their married children or married children too dependent on parents.

You may be involved with someone and while you say we're just friends," you know it has become more than friendship. Are others raising a concern about how much you are communicating with a certain person or persons? ___ (This is usually a dead give-away that something is questionable.) Do not try to rationalize or defend a relationship you know is improper. This inevitably opens the door to Satan and leads you into ever deepening bondage. Did any of the listed scenarios describe a specific area in your life? ___

If you lack peace about any relationship, it is likely coming to your mind right now. If a face is coming to your mind, I can guarantee you one thing — I did not put it there! It is very likely that God is speaking to your heart. After honest reflection, list relationships that need repentance._____

_____

In confessing and forsaking improper relationships, let us confidently claim the forgiveness and power of Christ's grace. Before making any major changes in relationships, it might be wise to consult with a pastor or counselor. Make sure everyone involved has appropriate counseling and emotional support. We should never be rash or careless about any decision that affects others.

However, do not let the potential difficulty be an excuse for staying in a wrong relationship. Any large church can provide pastoral counseling to anyone who needs it. Even if you do not know anyone at the church, call the staff and they can provide counsel. Trust God for the grace to go forward and take the immediate steps of obedience. In Jesus' name and passion, pray the following prayers.

Day Thirteen Prayer Focus

☐ Ask God for complete honesty about any personal or online relationships that have gotten out of balance. Confess and forsake any patterns God reveals. Trust Jesus to give the determination and power to make the changes right now. (Romans 14:23; 1 Thessalonians 5:22)

☐ Plead for God's merciful grace on a nation and many churches that are under his righteous judgment (2 Chronicles 7:14; Psalm 85:4-7; Daniel 9:18-19; Hebrews 4:16; James 4:8-10; 1 Peter 4:17)

Day Fourteen — Becoming a Godly Husband and Dad

The fourteenth day devotion is unique in that it contains specific readings and reflective questions for husbands, wives, parents and children. *The idea is for participants to read **only** the sections that pertain to them* (i.e. fathers read the fathers section, moms read moms, parents, etc.) Each reader should simply skip to the categories that pertain to you and pray through those.

The Scriptures for each category reveal God's plumb line for husbands, wives, parents and children. No one can be right with God while ignoring damaged family relationships. Though none of us are anywhere near perfect, we can and must surrender to God's grace for change. Day Fourteen may well take longer because most will need to pray through more than one category. Please take a few extra moments. This subject is *far* too important to rush! Prayerfully work through the appropriate categories below.

God's special words to husbands and fathers: Ephesians 5:23(a), *"For the husband is the head of the wife, as also Christ is the head of the church..."* From this verse we see that God calls the husband to be the spiritual head of the home. He is responsible to give spiritual guidance and nurture. Every husband and father has a very special responsibility to God and to his family.

Ephesians 5:25 - *"Husbands, love your wives, just as Christ also loved the church and gave Himself for her."*

1 Peter 3:7 - *"Husbands, likewise, dwell with them with understanding, giving honor to the wife, as to the weaker vessel, and as being heirs together of the grace of life, that your prayers may not be hindered.*

God commands husbands to love their wives with a powerful, sacrificial love. He is to literally sacrifice himself to meet the needs of his wife. The husband is to give himself' to meet the physical, emotional and spiritual needs of his wife. In every way, he is to place the needs and welfare of his wife ahead of his own.

God instructs husbands to be very caring and sensitive to his wife's needs. A husband's uncaring, insensitive attitude toward his wife will inevitably hinder his ability to pray (1 Peter 3: 7). A godly husband will literally study the unique needs and desires of his wife. This includes physical, emotional, mental, financial and spiritual needs.

Ephesians 6:4 - *"and you fathers, do not provoke your children to wrath, but bring them up in the training and admonition of the Lord."*

The father is also commanded to relate to his children in loving spiritual guidance, not in anger or wrath. Discipline must be done with consistency and love. The father's great priority is the spiritual nurture and training of his family. While financial provision is certainly very important, the father's first responsibility is spiritual growth of his family. But let every man be encouraged! While none of us are anywhere near perfect, God will give us great grace for solid steps of growth.

Questions for Reflection: Husband, have you taken responsibility to lead your family in devotions and prayer? ____ Do you set a loving atmosphere of spiritual nurture and training? ____ Do you put your wife's needs and desires ahead of your own? ____ Do you study to understand and meet the unique emotional needs of your wife? ____ Have you made use of today's excellent books and videos on marriage? ____ Are you viewing or listening to anything you would not want your wife to know? ___ Do you have any relationships that are in any way inappropriate? ___ Are you talking (or emailing) in ways you would not want your spouse or children to see? __ Do you have any Facebook "friends" that have moved past the point of being fully appropriate? ___ (Emotional unfaithfulness can be just as real as that which is physical!)

Are you providing wise financial guidance and stewardship for the security of your family? ___ Are you guiding your children in spiritual growth and training? ___ Do you discipline your children with consistency and love? ___ Do you consistently talk to your children about spiritual values? ___ (A brief daily devotion alone can never replace the value of consistent conversation with your children about everyday life issues.)

Let no husband despair! If you honestly confess your failures, God will give you the powerful grace to change. Today, there are many good books and resources to help you. Don't be overwhelmed even though you may feel inept. God will bless even small steps toward fulfilling your spiritual responsibility. Husband, you can see a miracle in your family! List specific ways you need to change. _____

_____

_____

_____

Day Fourteen Prayer Focus for Husbands and Dads

📖 Confess and forsake all patterns of inadequate love, provision and spiritual leadership. Pray for the commitment and strength to be a godly husband and dad. Trust Jesus to be your wisdom and power to be a godly husband and dad. (Deuteronomy 6:6; Ephesians 5:25; 1 Peter 3:7)

📖 Pray for an explosion of first love passion for Christ and a deep burden for lost humanity (Matthew 5:6, 44, 22:37-39; Philippians 2:13; 1 John 4:7-11, 20-21; Revelation 2:1-4, 3:15)

Day Fourteen (continued) — Faithful Wives and Mothers

Ephesians 5:24, 33(b) - *"Therefore just as the church is subject to Christ, so let the wives be to their own husbands in everything... and the wife see that she respects her husband."*

1 Peter 3:3 - *"Do not let your adornment be merely outward— arranging the hair, wearing gold, or putting on fine apparel— rather let it be the hidden person of the heart, with the incorruptible beauty of a gentle and quiet spirit, which is very precious in the sight of God."*

The wife's submission does not mean the husband can be a harsh master or boss over her. They are equal partners in the grace of Christ. Rather, her submission is the loving and willing submission seen with Christ and His Church. Thus, a godly wife exhibits a beautiful spirit of humility, love and honor toward her husband. She is to have a "gentle and quiet" spirit.

Questions for Reflection: Wives, do you treat your husband with dishonor and disrespect? ___ Do you often point out his weaknesses and faults? ___ Do you patiently forgive and treat him kindly in spite of his shortcomings? ___ Do you ignore his needs and desires? ___ Have you grown careless with your health and appearance? ___ Do you have a rebellious spirit toward him? ___ Have you done all you can do to bring your attitude in line with the pattern God has set for you in Scripture? ___ Is your attitude one of thanksgiving and love or complaining and anger? ___

Do you have relationships that are in any way inappropriate? ___ Are you talking (or emailing) anyone in ways you would not want your spouse or children to see? ___ Do you have any Facebook "friends" that have moved past the point of being fully appropriate? ___ (Emotional unfaithfulness can be just as real as that which is physical!) List specific ways you need to change.

_____

_____

_____

_____

According to Scripture, the greatest way to see God change your husband is to bring *yourself* under God's pattern for a godly wife. (1 Peter 3:1-2) Wives don't give up on your husband or yourself. Don't make excuses by saying, "I just don't have a gentle and quiet personality." If you honestly surrender to God's pattern, you will see a miracle in your home!

As wives confess and forsake dishonoring husbands and neglecting family, they stand in the forgiveness and power of Christ's blood. From your heart, pray the following prayers.

> ### Day Fourteen Prayer Focus for Wives and Mothers
>
> 📖 Confess any lack of love, reverence or faithfulness. Pray for God's guidance to be a godly wife and mother. Trust Jesus to fill you with His own love, faithfulness for your family. (Proverbs 31; Ephesians 5:24, 33; 1 Peter 3:3)
>
> 📖 Cry out for deep brokenness, God-Seeking reverential fear and humble repentance to sweep God's people (Psalm 51:17; Proverbs 28:13; John 14:15; 2 Corinthians 7:1, 10; Ephesians 5:26-27; Hebrews 12:14)

Day Fourteen (continued) – Becoming Spirit-Empowered Parents

Deuteronomy 6:6-8 – *"And these words which I command you today shall be in your heart. You shall teach them diligently to your children, and shall talk of them when you sit in your house, when you walk by the way, when you lie down, and when you rise up. You shall bind them as a sign on your hand, and they shall be as frontlets between your eyes."*

Proverbs 22:6 – *"Train up a child in the way he should go, And when he is old he will not depart from it."*

Matthew 18:6 - *"But whoever causes one of these little ones who believe in Me to sin, it would be better for him if a millstone were hung around his neck, and he were drowned in the depth of the sea."*

Because children are incredibly perceptive, they usually pick up more from what parents do than what they say. Often without even realizing it, parents are modeling values and habits that have tragic effects on their children's development. Training up a child in the way he should go is more about daily example than occasionally sharing religious words.

Questions for Reflection: Parent, do you model excitement and joy about worshiping God? ___ Do you consistently express love for Christ's Church or a negative complaining attitude? ___ If your children are expressing a negative attitude toward God and His church, you may need to take a serious look at the attitudes you actually model before them.

Have you failed to consistently teach your children Scripture? ___ Do you fail to regularly pray with and for your children? ___ Have you abdicated your primary responsibility to teach your children at home and left it to the Church? ___ Have you failed to diligently protect your children from media and Internet wickedness? ___

Parents, do you lovingly and consistently communicate with each other? ___ Do you consistently take time to talk to your children? ___ Do you really listen when your children talk to you? ___ Do you respond with love and understanding or quickly become angry? ___ If your children are pulling away from you, ask God to reveal ways you may have caused it.

Parent, do you model moral purity by the things you talk about? ___ Have you demonstrated holiness by the things you watch or read? ___ Have you consistently communicated God's standards concerning sex and marriage to your children? ___ Do you communicate in a way that reveals understanding about their temptations and struggles? ___ Have you been approachable and loving? ___ If your children are moving towards immorality, ask God if there are ways you should examine your example. If they won't talk to you, ask God if you've contributed to the barrier.

Parent, do you consistently model honesty and respect for others? ___ Do you break speed laws or cheat on taxes? ___ Have you demonstrated the ability to readily admit your own sins and failures? ___ Do you readily admit your sins or do you make excuses? ___ If your children are demonstrating tendencies toward cheating or lying, you should seriously examine your own example.

Dear readers, by no means do I suggest that children's problems are automatically a result of parental failure! In fact, Satan frequently heaps false guilt on broken-hearted parents. Regardless of all efforts, our children still have a will of their own. We are not to blame for all their bad choices. However, as parents we must face the awesome power of our example. May God give us the honesty to confess ways we have failed our children by attitude and example.

In many cases, parents need to ask forgiveness of their children (even older or adult children). Humility and honesty will have an enormous healing effect on strained parent- child relationships. Some of the above questions were drawn by permission from **A Christian Parent's Checklist** by Shelia Jones (Email address SJonesAZ@aol.com)[16] List specific adjustments you need to make as a parent. _____

_____

_____

_____

As we confess and forsake our sins and failures as parents, let us ever place our trust in the perfect Father. Though there are no perfect parents, God's power makes up the gaps. For practical help with family prayer and power, please contact our office for the resource **Powerful Prayer for Every Family.**[17] Trust His grace and pray the following prayers from your heart.

Day Fourteen Prayer Focus for Parents

📖 Confess and forsake any patterns of error or neglect. Pray for God's grace for parenting your children into spiritual, emotional, physical and relational health. Trust Jesus as your grace and strength for godly parenting. (Deuteronomy 6:6-10; Proverbs 22:6; Matthew 18:6)

📖 Cry out for a mighty movement of fervent personal and corporate prayer with spirit-led fasting (2 Chronicles 7:14; Joel 1:14, 2:12-18; Matthew 6:16-18, 17:21, 21:13; Mark 11:17; Acts 2:1, 4:30-31; James 5:16)

Day Fourteen (continued) — Honor Your Parents

Ephesians 6:1-3 - *"Children, obey your parents in the Lord, for this is right. 'Honor your father and mother,' which is the first commandment with promise: 'that it may be well with you and you may live long on the earth.'"*

Old Testament law pronounced severe punishment on children who cursed or dishonored a parent. Modern society must relearn the extreme importance of honoring parents. Sadly, many in today's generation have reversed the principle of honoring one's parents. We must clearly understand that honoring parents does *not* stop when we leave home! As long as we live, they deserve our love and honor (and care in later life.) A vital part of honoring parents is not to neglect them when they are older.

Questions for Reflection: Children or teenagers, do you disobey your parents? ___ Do you often ignore their guidance? ___ Have you treated your parents with disrespect or anger? ___ Disrespect toward parents is a very serious sin before God. Young people, you cannot be right with God if you consistently disrespect your parents. As adults, we too must ask whether we are honoring our elderly parents. Do you neglect to call and visit your aged parents? ___ Do you neglect your Mother and Father by failing to give them consistent time and attention? ___ Are you neglecting them emotionally or financially? ___ Do you fail to help them with needs around their home? ___ Are there unresolved harsh words or feelings between you and your parents? ___ Have you truly sought to make it right? ___ Remember, no one who mistreats or neglects a parent can be fully right with God! List specific ways you need to change.

_____

_____

_____

Day Fourteen Prayer Focus for Honoring Parents

📖 Confess and forsake any patterns of dishonor, disobedience, resentment or neglect. Ask God for the determination and power to honor, obey and care for our parents. Trust Jesus for the grace and love to properly honor your parents. (Ephesians 6:1-3)

📖 Plead for God's powerful manifest presence, a restraining of evil and a mighty outpouring of His Spirit (Exodus 33:15; 1 Kings 8:11; Isaiah 59:19; Zechariah 4:6; Acts 1:8, 2:1-2, 4:31)

Week Three

My Covenant to Lasting Obedience
The Heart of First Love Surrender

*T*his third week brings us to the very heart of a genuine return to God. It is also the heart of new fullness and power in Christ. To experience full fellowship, joy and power, the Lord *requires* far more than general confession or temporary events. We are to return *to* Christ in specific covenants of lasting obedience. Modern efforts at prayer and repentance often fall short because they are too general and temporary. In this week's devotions and prayers, readers will embrace the essence of lasting change.

The heart of first love surrender is an *intentional, Spirit-empowered commitment* to walk in specific steps of ongoing obedience. In the next seven days, I highlight four commitments (or covenants) that are central to lasting obedience and power. The strategic covenants are essential for Christ's full Lordship in a believer's life. Readers will experience full power and renewal through embracing the covenants for lasting change.

Above all, we embrace the covenants as a love relationship by grace through faith, *not* legalism or self-reliance. Each covenant includes a practical tool to help believers experience God in lasting change. The tools are four Bible inserts that equip believers to walk in effective ongoing obedience. Approach this week with great confidence and hope. By God's grace, we *can* return to Him in lasting revival!

Day Fifteen — Repentance from Idolatry
Prioritizing Christ and His Church

Exodus 20:2(a)-3 - *"I am the Lord your God....you shall have no other gods before Me."*

Matthew 6:24 - *"No man can serve two masters: for either he will hate the one and love the other, or else he will be loyal to the one, and despise the other. You cannot serve God and money."*

Matthew 13:22 – *"Now he who received seed among the thorns is he who hears the word, and the cares of this world and the deceitfulness of riches choke the word, and he becomes unfruitful."*

Though today most people do not bow to some carved image, we may commonly commit the sin of idolatry. (An idol is *anything* we place ahead of God and His service). The Bible calls these "idols of the heart." (Ezekiel 14:1-8)

In Matthew 13:22, Jesus stated that the "deceitfulness of riches and cares of this life" choke out God's word (and will) in their lives. In other words, daily cares move ahead of knowing and serving God. According to Scripture, this is nothing short of idolatry! While God certainly understands that we have many responsibilities in daily life, He gives the grace to keep them balanced. Sadly, many have totally abandoned that balance. For vast numbers, Christ and His Church are more a sideline than first priority.

Victory Over "Me Generation" Idolatry

More and more churches are witnessing an unprecedented shortage of givers, attendees and workers. In spite of many excuses, the primary reason is a major lack of commitment among church members. Many churches and ministries can barely function because so many hardly attend even once a week, give only sporadically and in low amounts.

While various reasons are offered, the central reality is that everything else comes ahead of Christ and His Church. A question to ponder is "how much would the early Church have spread if the members had barely attended an hour every week or so." What if they had not had the passion to meet for intense prayer and discipleship three or four times a week? In all likelihood, Christianity would never have survived the first century and our churches would not exist! There is little question that many modern believers need a major adjustment in commitment to Christ's Church. According to God's word, real life and joy is putting Jesus first. When we do, everything else is successful. (Matthew 6:33) Until we do, we are in the bondage of idolatry.

Questions for Reflection: Have you transgressed God's first commandment by placing other things ahead of God? ___ Have other things or people crowded out your worship and service to God? ___ Do you worship and serve God only if everything else is done first? ___ Has your work and financial gain actually become your god? ___ Have you voted for politicians who promote ungodly principles just because they're in your political party? ___ If so, you have definitely placed human politics over God and Scripture. Such practice amounts to plain idolatry.

Do you spend far more time on the Internet or watching television than in Bible reading and prayer? ___ Have you placed your family ahead of God? (The best way to lose a family is to place them ahead of God.) ___ Does recreation or some hobby take precedence over God's service? ___ Have you become one who perpetually "visits" various churches but never commits as a contributing, consistent part of the Body? ___ (As long as we are "visiting" we can avoid the responsibilities of true church membership.)

If all church members followed your example of service, how strong would be the ministry of your church? ___ Would there be a Sunday or Wednesday evening service if everyone attended like you? ___ Would there be an outreach or prayer ministry? ___ Who or what is really number one in your life? According to Scripture, *no* believer has the right to be a "part-time" Christian or an "uncommitted" church member. (Matthew 16:24; Luke 6:46, 14:26) Confess and forsake ways you have allowed other things to come before God. Believe Him to give you a genuine heart of worship. In Jesus' name, lift these petitions to God.

Day Fifteen Prayer Focus

📖 Confess and forsake all patterns of letting other things come before Christ and kingdom service. (Be specific.) Ask God to help you place Christ and His Church as your first priority. Trust Jesus for the determination and power to lay aside all idolatry. (Luke 14:26-30)

📖 Pray for a burning passion for evangelism, discipleship and missions to sweep God's people (Matthew 24:14, 28:18-20; Luke 19:10; Acts 1:8; Romans 9:1-3)

Day Sixteen — Repentance from Robbing God

Becoming True "Grace Givers"

Malachi 3:8-10- *"Will a man rob God? Yet you have robbed Me! But you say, 'In what way have we robbed You? In tithes and offerings. You are cursed with a curse, For you have robbed Me, even this whole nation. Bring you all the tithes into the storehouse, That there may be food in My house, and try Me now in this,' says the Lord of hosts, 'If I will not open for you the windows of heaven, And pour out for you a blessing, That there will not be room enough to receive it."*

God has commanded His children to give tithes and offerings. Failure to at least tithe is so serious, God calls it robbery and spiritual idolatry. Because of blatant financial disobedience, many believers are not filled with the Holy Spirit. They forfeit much of God's full blessing. To refuse to tithe is to place money and things ahead of God.

For those who say "tithing is Old Testament and we are under grace," remember Jesus words about the new covenant. Jesus said His grace standard is always much "more" than the law. In other words, tithing is the lowest requirement. True grace giving consistently and cheerfully *exceeds* the basic requirement of the law. (Matthew 5:33-42)

Mark this well — being "under grace" is no excuse to avoid giving even the most basic tithe for Christ's kingdom! If someone says, "I'm a grace giver" and consistently gives less than a tithe, they are deceiving themselves about the meaning of grace. If someone is too uncommitted to at least tithe, they should be very careful about using "grace" as an excuse. Such patterns are the very opposite of real grace.

Beyond question, generous and consistent giving is *still* God's command to His people. In essence, failing to give even a tithe is nothing less than common thievery against the God who has given everything for us. (Malachi 3:8) It is deeply disturbing that many think nothing of giving a fifteen percent tip to a restaurant waiter, yet find ten percent too much for the Giver of all life. (What does this say about priorities?)[18] Most would not dare defraud the IRS; yet think nothing of defrauding God every week in His own house of worship. What does this say about our fear and reverence of God?

Questions for Reflection: Have you been honest to fully tithe your time and talents to God? ___ Have you been honest in calculating your tithe or have you tithed from the leftovers rather than the fast fruits of your income? ___ (Do you give God what's left over after everyone else gets theirs?) ___

Jesus Christ cannot be Lord of your life if He is not Lord of your finances. Have you figured the tithe to the penny but been stingy with any offerings beyond the tithe? ___ Would you be willing to give far more than a tithe if God leads you? ___ After all, a tithe is the bare minimum God requires. How can we not joyfully give far more than the bare minimum? ___

Spirit-filled believers give cheerfully, generously and sacrificially. Carnal believers put money and things ahead of God. If you sense God's conviction about finances, obey Him now. Friend, you will quickly discover you cannot out-give God! He will give back to you far more than you could ever give to Him (Luke 6:38).

As we confess and forsake our sins of withholding tithes and offerings from God, let us rejoice in the greatness of His grace. (Romans 8:1; 1 John 1:9) His mercy is higher than the heavens!

Trusting His fullness and grace, pray these prayers from your heart.

Day Sixteen Prayer Focus

📖 Confess and forsake all patterns of the idolatry of placing money and things ahead of God. Ask God for the honesty to acknowledge ways you are robbing Him by neglect of tithes and offerings. Trust Jesus for the heart to give generously out of faith and love, not duty. (Malachi 3:8-10; Luke 6:46)

📖 Plead for Church leaders filled with holy boldness, fervent prayer, spiritual power and strong scripture focus (1 Corinthians 2:4; 1 Timothy 3:1-2; 2 Timothy 1:6-)

Day Seventeen —My Covenant to Abide in Christ

Daily Prayer, Scripture and Surrender

Psalms 27:8 – *"When You said, "Seek My face," My heart said to You, "Your face, LORD, I will seek."*

John 15:4-5 - *"Abide in me, and I in you. As the branch cannot bear fruit of itself, unless it abides in the vine, neither can you, unless you abide in Me. I am the vine, you are the branches. He that abides in Me, and I in him, bears much fruit; for without Me you can do nothing."*

James 4:8, 5:16b – *"Draw near to God and He will draw near to you. Cleanse your hands, you sinners; and purify your hearts, you double-minded......The effective, fervent prayer of a righteous man avails much."*

In many ways, today's focus is the most essential element of returning to God in lasting obedience. The greatest reason most believers struggle is seriously inadequate patterns of daily prayer, Bible reading and surrender to Christ's Lordship. In too many modern prayer efforts, little is done to deepen believers' *ongoing* daily pattern of prayer and surrender. For this reason, lasting fruit and power are often quite limited. If solemn assemblies and prayer emphases do not change believers' ongoing prayer lives, whatever cleansing they might experience is unlikely to last.

The most crucial ways we abide in Jesus are regular Bible reading, deep surrender and kingdom-centered prayer. It is virtually impossible to live in full spiritual power without effective daily prayer and Scripture! (John 15:4-7) Neglecting significant time with God greatly limits spiritual growth and power.[19] Tragically, many have bought into the unbiblical notion that all one needs is a brief two or three minute daily devotion. While that may sound appealing to many in today's society, it is definitely not the pattern of Scripture and history.

Rejecting Today's "Spiritual Inoculation" Syndrome

Excessive shallowness in prayer and surrender are the major reasons spiritual power is lacking in many lives. In many ways, it is a form of "spiritual inoculation." In other words, we can embrace such shallow, weakened forms of prayer, we are prevented from experiencing God's full closeness and power. While this pattern is largely unconscious and unintended, it is all-too common among modern believers. Rather than a watered-down Americanized substitute, we must return to fully empowered biblical prayer. Shallow prayers are arguably the greatest reasons for today's unprecedented spiritual decline.

Mark this well—any serious return to God *requires* a covenant to walk with Christ in deeper daily prayer and surrender. In spite of today's micro-sound bite mindset, there simply are no "short-cuts" to fullest biblical power and intimacy with Jesus. New Testament power requires New Testament-type prayer! While this powerful prayer does not mean some legalistic formula or ritual, it does mean deeper patterns than most believers now practice. But be assured — deep daily prayer and surrender are *not* out of reach. Neither does it take exorbitant time!

The key to effective abiding in Jesus is to make that relationship your top priority. You cannot merely say, "I will *try* to give God more time." You have to actually set your alarm clock or go into your quiet place and *do* it! For most believers, this means making a commitment to strengthen four elements in their daily prayer and Scripture patterns.

(1) To embrace designated prayer times that are more consistent and not as rushed. (Just going from four or five minutes to twenty or thirty can *revolutionize* a prayer life!) (2) In your prayer time, frequently include at least five to ten minutes of deeper cleansing and yielding to Christ's Lordship. (3) Shift your prayers to a greater focus on eternal issues. (4) Add a few moments of meditative listening to God's voice through His word.

At this juncture, some readers might be feeling a bit overwhelmed. Some are likely wondering if they can really make these changes or measure up to New Testament prayer. Forget such thoughts! *First*, God's grace and patience are sufficient. *Second*, **Appendices B** and **C** contain all you need for your daily journey. Best of all, the two appendices are brief and easy to use. They are also available as practical inserts believers can keep right in their Bible! Anyone can use these to develop powerful prayer patterns.

The central purpose of today's devotion is to help each reader make a covenant to more effectively abide in Christ. For help that is more extensive than **Appendices B** and **C**, the practical book, **How to Develop a Powerful Prayer Life** contains all you need for powerful daily closeness with Jesus. Be assured — God's grace is sufficient and you *can* learn to abide in Christ! Let the following reflective questions guide you to a whole new walk with God. It will make an enormous difference in every area of your life.

Questions for Reflection: Do you spend substantial time in consistent Bible reading and effective prayer? ___ (This must be more than a two or three minute devotion.) Indeed, how could we expect to experience genuine worship, thorough confession, biblical petitions and serious intercession in only four or five minutes a day? ___ Have you been too "busy" to give God significant time? ___ Remember, you will never be spiritually stronger than the strength and quality of your personal time with God in Scripture and prayer. You must be willing to spend significant daily time with God (at least 20-40 minutes). Have you neglected to abide in a close, consistent relationship with Christ? ___ Confess and forsake the debilitating sin of neglecting significant Bible reading and prayer. These elements are the very heart of your closeness and power in Jesus.

As you covenant to give more time to daily prayer and surrender, be specific about "how and when" you will do it. Vague pledges usually mean nothing. For many, this will mean setting a clock earlier and deciding the specific steps of your new pattern. If stronger prayer is to become a reality, your commitment must be definite and specific. Trusting God's grace, make the following covenant to abide in Christ.

My Covenant to Abide in Christ — Lord, by Your grace and Spirit, I covenant to dedicate more significant time to reading Scripture, focused prayer, deeper surrender and careful listening to Your voice.

As we confess and forsake our failure to faithfully draw near to God in prayer, let us ever place our sole trust in the *"author and finisher of our faith."* (Hebrews 12:2) Lift the following prayers to the throne of grace.

Day Seventeen Prayer Focus

In your own words, pray something like the following prayer. "Lord, forgive me for spending too little time in Your word and prayer. By Your grace and Spirit, I will make significant time for stronger prayer, deeper cleansing and full yielding of my heart. I covenant to live in Your lordship and fullness." (Psalm 66:18; John 15:4-8; James 5:16)

Cry out for supernatural love and unity to sweep churches, denominations and families. Revival involves deep love and unity. (John 13:34-35, 15:12, 17:20-22; Acts 2:1, 42-47; 1 Corinthians 1:10; Ephesians 4:29-32)

Day Eighteen — My Covenant to Witness, Embrace Missions and Pray for Spiritual Awakening

Psalm 85:6 – *"Will You not revive us again, That Your people may rejoice in You?"*

Ezekiel 3:18 – *"When I say to the wicked, 'You shall surely die,' and you give him no warning, nor speak to warn the wicked from his wicked way, to save his life, that same wicked man shall die in his iniquity; but his blood I will require at your hand."*

Matthew 28:18-20 – *"And Jesus came and spoke to them, saying, "All authority has been given to Me in heaven and on earth. Go therefore and make disciples of all the nations, baptizing them in the name of the Father and of the Son and of the Holy Spirit, teaching them to observe all things that I have commanded you; and lo, I am with you always, even to the end of the age."*

Acts 1:8- *"But you shall receive power when the Holy Spirit has come upon you; and you shall be witnesses unto Me in Jerusalem, and in all Judea and in Samaria, and to the end of the earth."*

If Jesus is truly your Lord, *His* first priorities must become *your* first priority. Walking under Christ's Lordship *requires* a personal commitment to His central heart priorities. (Luke 6:46) There is no question that witnessing, supporting missions and praying for spiritual awakening are at the very top of Christ's priorities for His people. Through these priorities, Christ's kingdom expands and God is most glorified.

It is virtually *impossible* for anyone to genuinely return to God and ignore His great priorities in their daily life. Beyond question, God has called *all* His children to witness, support missions and pray for revival and awakening. While there are certainly variations in how each of us practice these priorities, *all* must prioritize them. Believers, if we fail to witness, we literally become responsible for the lost condition of those around us. According to Scripture, *"their blood is then on our hands."* (Ezekiel 3:18)

It is also unacceptable to neglect missions involvement and/or fail to pray for revival and spiritual awakening. Great revivals come only one way — by the consistent fervent prayers of God's people. Thus, if we fail to embrace at least some missions involvement and prayer for spiritual awakening, we are part of today's problem. Surveys indicate many Christians do not pray consistently for revival and spiritual awakening.* These same surveys even show surprising numbers of leaders do not regularly pray for this vital issue.

Thankfully, there are powerful and practical ways *every* believer can learn to embrace missions and pray for spiritual awakening. Though we cannot all physically go and do missions, we can all at least give and pray. And while we are not all called to do evangelism and missions exactly the same way, *all* believers must embrace the commitment to at least pray.

In today's devotion, believers are asked to make a covenant to pray for lost people, missions and spiritual awakening. In **Appendices D** and **E**, I provide Covenant and Prayer Guides that are biblical, practical and powerful. While believers are not required to pray through these every day, even periodically helps put us in the center of God's will. The covenants are also available as practical prayer guides to keep in a Bible.

One thing is certain — *no one* can truly surrender to Christ and not embrace His heart priorities. But again, let no one be intimidated. As believers covenant to pray for evangelism, missions and spiritual awakening, God fills them with Himself! He also reveals ways we can give and do missions. Doing and praying God's priorities bring a joy and power beyond description! As participants work through the following Questions for Reflection, embrace the covenants to pray for the lost, missions and spiritual awakening. (**Appendices D** and **E** contain the practical covenants with prayer guides.)

Questions for Reflection: Have you made a prayer list of people you consistently encounter in your daily course of life (store clerks, gas station attendants, work mates, classmates, neighbors, etc.)? ___ Do you pray for them on a fairly regular basis? ___ Do you seek to show them special kindness? ___ Do you witness to them about Christ? ___ Do you leave gospel tracts in places you frequent? ___

To be ashamed of Christ is a grievous sin against God. The sin of silence is one of our greatest failures! (Mark 8:38) To love and surrender to Jesus, we must embrace His primary heart purposes. For this reason, every believer should maintain a list of at least some lost people for whom they pray regularly. All believers should pray for and witness to those with whom they have some connection (neighbors, classmates, family, etc.).

Have you failed to prioritize giving and praying for missions? ____ Is prayer for revival and spiritual awakening neglected in your prayer life? ___ Remember, Jesus cannot be Lord of any life that neglects the three issues in this devotion. If you have failed God, confess this sin now. To fail to pray effectively for revival is to neglect God's heart and purpose. Even as our nation experiences much worse catastrophes, God's remnant can be revived! Commit to become a consistent intercessor and faithful witness. **Appendices D** and **E** show exactly how. From your heart embrace the following covenant.

My Covenant to Pray for the Lost, Missions and Spiritual Awakening — Lord, by Your grace and Spirit, I covenant to consistently pray for lost people, missions and spiritual awakening. I also covenant to spread Your kingdom and glory by my resources and tithe.

As we confess our failure to obey Christ's great commission and our lack of compassion for lost souls all around us, as we endeavor to obey Him with a whole heart, let us rejoice in God's full acceptance for us and for others. (Romans 8:1; 1 John 1:9) His mercy is higher than the heavens! Lift the following prayers to God.

Day Eighteen Prayer Focus

- Confess and forsake any failure to pray for the lost, missions and spiritual awakening. Embrace the personal covenant to pray for (and witness to) the lost and for global spiritual awakening. (Psalm 51:17; Proverbs 28:13; John 14:15; 2 Corinthians 7:1, 10; Ephesians 5:26-27; Hebrews 12:14)

- Pray for powerful faith, pure motives and godly wisdom in seasons of judgment. (Joshua 1:9; Jeremiah 29:16-18, 45:5; Acts 4:29-31; Matthew 6:33, 9:29, 16:18, 17:20; Mark 9:23, 11:22-24; 2 Timothy 1:7; James 4:1-4)

Day Nineteen — Dying to Self and Embracing the Cross

Overcoming Delayed Obedience and False Repentance

Matthew 16:24-25 - *"If any man will come after me, let him deny himself and take up his cross, and follow me. For whoever desires to save his life will lose it, but whoever loses his life for My sake will find it."*

Mark 8:35 - *"For whosoever will save his life shall lose it; but whosoever shall lose his life for my sake and the gospel's, the same shall save it."*

Luke 6:46 - *"But why do you call me 'Lord,' and not do the things which I say?"*

Romans 14:23b - *"If I do anything without a firm conviction it is God's will, it is for me a sin."* (author's paraphrase)

Hebrews 12:1 – *"Therefore we also, since we are surrounded by so great a cloud of witnesses, let us lay aside every weight, and the sin which so easily ensnares us, and let us run with endurance the race that is set before us."*

A most critical area of returning to God is surrender of our self-will and personal preferences. While "dying to self" may sound strange to many in our day, it is essential to Christ being fully Lord in our daily lives. It deals with our acknowledgement that God is God and deserves our total love and surrender. Indeed, we are *"not our own and have been bought with a price."* (1 Corinthians 6:19-20) Humbling ourselves before God and others is crucial to surrendering to Christ. Jesus said *no one* can be His disciple without dying to self. (Matthew 16:24)

Dying to self does not always mean rejecting an actual sin. It could simply be a "weight" (or personal preference) that needs to be released. (Hebrews 12:1) It could well be something that is not actually sinful but simply occupies too much of our affection, energy or time. Some common examples are: hobbies, sports, work, relationships, our own conveniences, personal preferences, comforts, money, appearance, etc. In such cases, the issue may not be an overt sin, but has simply gotten out of balance.

The intentional, specific surrender of *everything* is how we daily "die to self." Total surrender is the meaning of fully "embracing the cross." (Matthew 16:24-27) It is also something we must do *daily*. (Luke 9:23; 1 Corinthians 15:31) Yet, just saying "I surrender everything" is usually a far cry from actually doing it. Meaningful surrender requires deep, point by point surrender. (The **Questions for Reflection** help guide believers to meaningful surrender.)

While of course, surrender is all by God's grace and Spirit, we must nonetheless "choose" to embrace deep, daily yielding. (2 Corinthians 7:1; Colossians 1:27) By surrendering self, we experience a glorious fullness of Christ flowing through our lives. Surrendering self relates to who is truly Lord (or boss) of our lives. For extensive help with this subject, check out **Living the Crucified Life:** *"The Power of Dying to Self"* by Gregory Frizzell.

Victory Over "Delayed Obedience" and "False Repentance"

Common forms of avoiding the cross are today's patterns of "delayed obedience" and "false repentance." In these subtle but real conditions, believers may confess certain sins but fail to truly repent or fully obey. Through self-deceptive reasonings they in essence "put off" repentance and/or make excuses for remaining partially in the sin.

As perhaps no other area, sins of self-will, delayed obedience and unyieldedness are the most subtle and unrecognized. As humans, we can be very adept at deceiving ourselves and justifying a lack of full surrender. But fear not — Jesus provides the full grace and power to yield to His Lordship! (Philippians 2:13) This section guides readers into complete surrender. The reflective questions help us recognize self-deceptive reasonings that are preventing our full surrender. After each of the following questions, pause for God to speak. Mark areas that need confession and repentance. Fully confess and forsake whatever God reveals. And remember this — by His grace you *can* repent!

Questions for Reflection — Do you continue to practice certain things though there is nagging guilt or uncertainty? ___ Do you sense there are issues about which you are delaying to embrace God's full will? ___ Do you often have to rationalize to try and convince yourself something is right when deep in your heart there is nagging doubt? ___ Do you find yourself repeatedly confessing the same three or four sins yet there is little real improvement? ___ (In essence, this is abusing God's grace by *"treading on the blood of Christ and ...treating it* (grace) *lightly."* Hebrews 10:26-28)

Is there some challenging area of surrender about which you pretend not to know what God is saying, yet you really have a fairly good idea? ___ Regarding some sin, have you used the excuse of delayed repentance by saying "I am working on this weakness." (Yet, you have been "working" on it for months and years with little or no progress.) This is proof positive you are deceiving yourself with false repentance. (Proverbs 28:13)

Is there any area of service you should be doing, yet you are not? ___ Have you let fear or inconvenience stop you from fully obeying some direction from God? ___ Are you often too proud to openly humble yourself, confess failure and ask forgiveness? ___

Do you become quickly angry and resentful when you are corrected, disappointed or slighted? ___ Have you profaned God's name by some outward display of anger, compromise or disobedience? ___ (A single act of rash public disobedience robbed God of glory and kept Moses from completing his full life's work.) Have you robbed God of glory by trying to live and serve Him in your own strength and wisdom? ___ All of the above issues reveal unyielded self-will.

Carefully review any points needing deeper surrender. Resolve now to put off self-will and wholly surrender to Christ's Lordship. Clearly identify your specific points of rebellion and self-will. Trust Jesus to help you yield your personal comforts, conveniences, preferences and will. List your specific steps for change. _____

_____

_____

_____

As you have confessed and forsaken the sins God revealed, rest confidently in His promise of complete forgiveness. *"He that covers his sins shall not prosper; but who confesses and forsakes them shall have mercy."* (Proverbs 28:13) *"If we confess our sins, He is faithful and just to forgive us our sins and to cleanse us from all unrighteousness."* (1 John 1:9)

Day Nineteen Prayer Focus

📖 Ask God for total honesty about ways you have not fully died to self. Confess and forsake the specific areas you need to yield. Trust Jesus for the grace and will to fully die to self and yielding to His Lordship. Believe Him for the fullness and power of the Holy Spirit. (Mark 8:35; Luke 6:46, 14:27)

📖 Plead for churches to fully proclaim Christ's preeminence, Calvary's cross and true new-birth conversion (John 3:3, 13:32, 16:8-14; Acts 4:12; Romans 6:1-14; Philippians 2:5-11; Colossians 1:9-18)

Day Twenty — Surrendering to All God Said in the Preceding Days

In many ways, today's devotion is most pivotal. We will ask God to help us embrace all He has said over the last nineteen days. Again, the Lord desires much more than general confession. **He desires specific repentance and a lasting new beginning**. (Proverbs 28:13) We must surrender the specific areas that need change. By so doing, God can fill us with awesome spiritual power and growth. To help with the process, I condensed each day's devotion into its central theme and a prayer of surrender.

Prayerfully consider each day's subject for issues God may reveal. Please be aware that today's devotion will take longer than some previous. Take your time and do not rush. After each day's prayer, I provide a blank space to write any specific steps for change. (Obviously, you use your own words.)

As readers reflect on the nineteen previous areas, let none be discouraged or overwhelmed. Focus on your few areas that most need to change. Our Lord surely knows we are imperfect and continually need His grace. Remember that we are wholly accepted in Christ's righteousness. (Ephesians 1:6) Through His grace, we are being transformed in His image! (Romans 12:1-2)

Day One -
First Love Passion for God — Blessed Lord, I repent from all lukewarmness — I commit my life to a burning first love passion for God and Christ.

_____

_____

Day Two –
Reverential Fear and Awe of God — Lord God, I repent of all irreverence — I commit my heart to hallow and reverence Your name in every area of life

_____

_____

Day Three –
A God-Seeking Life—Father God, I repent of failing to fervently seek You in ever-deeper knowledge — I covenant to frequently pray and meditate on Your attributes and names

_____

_____

Day Four –
Worship as My Lifestyle — Lord Jesus, I repent from shallow, insincere worship — I commit my whole life to be a reflection of Your worship

_____

_____

Day Five –   *Clean Hands and Pure Hearts* — Holy God, I repent from all impurity and lust — I wholly commit myself to purity of mind and heart

_____

_____

Day Six –   *Brokenness and Humility* — Lord of Glory, I repent of all my pride and prejudice — I surrender to deep brokenness and humility

_____

_____

Day Seven –   *Boldness, Courage and Faith* — Faithful God, I repent of doubt, fear and timidity — By Your grace I embrace holy boldness, courage and faith _____

_____

Day Eight –   *Love and Unity* — Gracious God, I repent of anger, bitterness and division — I embrace kindness, love and unity for Your glory _____

_____

Day Nine –   *Kingdom-Minded Values* — Lord of Lords, I repent from greed and worldliness — I covenant to seek first Your kingdom and righteousness

_____

_____

Day Ten –   *Godly Speech and Cyberspace* — Holy God, I repent from sinful speech, emails, tweets or texts — I wholly surrender my tongue and keypad to Your Lordship

_____

_____

Day Eleven -   *Reconciled Relationships* — God of Peace, I surrender all of my broken relationships — I commit to seek reconciliation with all I have offended

_____

_____

Day Twelve –   *Love and Forgiveness* — Lord of Grace, I repent from all bitterness and unforgiveness — I fully forgive all who have wronged me

_____

_____

Day Thirteen –   *Godly Relationships* — Blessed Lord, I repent from improper relationships — I commit to godly balance in all personal and online relations with others

_____

_____

Day Fourteen –   *A Godly Husband and Father* — Heavenly Father, I repent of neglecting my responsibilities as a Christian husband and father — I embrace all of Your patterns and commands for my home

_____

_____

Day Fourteen –   *A Godly Wife and Mother* — Lord Jesus, I repent of my neglect as a Christian wife and mother — I fully embrace all of Your patterns and commands for my home

_____

_____

Day Fourteen –   *Christian Parents* — God of Grace, I repent from neglecting my responsibilities as a Christian parent — I wholly embrace Your patterns and priorities for parents

_____

_____

Day Fourteen –   *Godly Children* — Blessed Father, I repent from any disobedience, neglect or dishonor to my parents — By Your grace, I embrace a right relationship with my parents

_____

_____

Day Fifteen –   *Neglect of Christ's Church and Service* — Lord Jesus, I repent from the idolatry of neglecting Your Church and Christian service — I commit to Jesus and His Church as my first priority

_____

_____

Day Sixteen –   *Godly Giving*—Lord and Savior, I repent from robbing You by withholding Your tithe — I commit to grace giving, tithes and offerings

_____

_____

Day Seventeen –   *Daily Abiding in Christ's Fullness* — Father God, I repent of my failure to daily abide in Christ — By Your grace, I embrace effective prayer, Scripture meditation and full daily surrender _____

_____

Day Eighteen –   *Evangelism, Discipleship, Missions and Spiritual Awakening* — Holy Lord, I repent from my neglect of discipleship, witnessing, missions and prayer for spiritual awakening — By Your grace, I embrace discipleship, missions and prayer for spiritual awakening

_____

_____

Day Nineteen —   *Dying to Self* — Sovereign God, I repent of self-will and false surrender — By Your power, I die to myself, embrace Christ's cross and surrender to full loving obedience

_____

_____

Surrendering My Whole Life to Christ's Lordship
The Essence of Lifestyle Worship

After reflecting on your specific points of surrender, *thank God* for His full forgiveness and grace. As you now surrender, be specific in the things you are forsaking and your steps of obedience. Do not be overwhelmed — the Lord knows we are all imperfect. In your own words, simply talk to God and freshly surrender your life to Jesus.

Day Twenty Prayer Focus

📖 Confess and forsake areas about which God has convicted your heart. Praise God for His grace and for Christ as your life and power. In a prayer from your heart, surrender your entire life to the Lordship of Jesus and glory of God. Trust the Lord to fill you with the Holy Spirit. (Romans 6:6-14; Galatians 2:20; Ephesians 5:18)

📖 Cry out for an explosion of sound biblical doctrine and theology with full exaltation of God's glory and grace (1 Chronicles 29:10-13; Isaiah 42:8; Acts 20:27; 1 Corinthians 1:29; Ephesians 1:3-6, 2:7-9; 1 Timothy 1:17)

Day Twenty-One — My Covenant to Lasting Obedience and First Love Passion

Luke 6:46 – *"But why do you call Me 'Lord, Lord,' and do not do the things which I say?"*

John 14:15 – *"If you love Me, keep My commandments."*

1 John 5:3 – *"For this is the love of God, that we keep His commandments. And His commandments are not burdensome."*

Revelation 2:4 – *"Nevertheless I have this against you, that you have left your first love."*

On this final day, we embrace a very specific covenant to walk with God in lasting first love obedience. On day twenty, we over-viewed all major points of repentance to which God spoke. Today, I present a Bible-based covenant for returning to God in new obedience. It is crucial to understand that true love to God means a concrete commitment to *ongoing* obedience. While we embrace this covenant as a love relationship by grace, we must nonetheless embrace the specific lasting changes!

My Covenant to Return to God consists of the seven heart commitments the Lord desires from His people. The seven points are the very essence of first love for God and full surrender to Christ's Lordship. They are the heart of sweeping revival and spiritual awakening. Without these seven points of commitments, it is *impossible* to return to God in full New Testament power.

The *first* three covenant points are (1) our heart passion and reverence for God, (2) our covenant to purity and holiness and (3) embracing right relationships with others. These first three commitments form the essential foundations of lifestyle worship, full surrender and Holy Spirit empowerment.

The *last* four covenant points are the "outward patterns" of walking daily in Jesus' Lordship. These outward practices are (1) deep daily cleansing and yielding, (2) effectively abiding in prayer and Scripture, (3) prayer and involvement in evangelism and missions, (4) praying for revival and spiritual awakening.

Return to Me is unique in that believers not only make a specific covenant, they embrace practical tools for daily living it out. For the living out of our covenant to God **Appendices A, B, C, D** and **E** were created as practical tools. Believers can put these tools right in their Bibles or devotion books. While of course, no one is required to legalistically use all every day, even periodic use will make an enormous difference!

Listed on page 93 is **My Covenant to Return to God.** Prayerfully read it and decide if this is what you desire to say to God. While of course, none of us could pledge to perfection, we can commit to embrace the seven points as our central purpose. Prayerfully read the covenant on the next page and decide if this represents the commitment you desire to give to God. While not claiming you will be perfect, you are prepared to embrace first love and deeper obedience. After reading the seven point covenant on the adjacent page, prayerfully make the following commitment trusting in God's grace and strength.

By God's grace and Spirit, I embrace **My Covenant to Return to God.** (In your own words pray through each of the seven points of the covenant.) If you have made this covenant, sign and date on the space provided.

_____

Date: _____

My Covenant to Return to God
"The Pledge to Lasting, First Love Surrender"
(Psalm 27:8; Zechariah 1:3)

1. Father God, I renounce all lukewarmness and lack of spiritual passion. By Your grace and Spirit I covenant to love, revere and seek You with all my heart. I covenant to love my neighbor as myself and bless my enemies. (Ecclesiastes 12:13; Matthew 22:37-39)

2. Lord Jesus, I repent of all anger, impurity, lust and pride. By Your grace and Spirit, I covenant to walk with clean hands, a pure heart and godly attitudes for Your glory. (Matthew 5:8; John 13:34; 1 Peter 5:5)

3. Heavenly Father, I repent of all unforgiveness and broken relationships. By Your grace and Spirit, I pledge to seek forgiveness of all I have offended and fully forgive all who have offended me. (Matthew 5:23-24, 6:14-15, 18:35)

4. Blessed Savior, I repent of neglecting Your word and prayer. By Your grace and Spirit, I covenant to daily abide in Your word, prayer and spiritual fullness. (John 15:4-15; Ephesians 5:18)

5. Holy God, I repent of shallow confession and surface yielding of my life. By Your grace and Spirit, I covenant to walk in full repentance and ever-deeper yielding to Christ's Lordship. (Psalm 66:16: Luke 6:46)

6. Holy Father, I repent of lukewarmness in evangelism and missions. By Your grace and Spirit, I covenant to consistently give, labor and pray for lost people, missions and kingdom growth. (Matthew 28:18-20; Acts 1:8)

7. Sovereign Lord, I repent of my failure to pray and labor for revival and spiritual awakening. By Your grace and Spirit, I covenant to consistently pray for powerful revival in the Church, spiritual awakening and evangelistic harvest for Christ's eternal worship. (Psalm 85:6; Isaiah 43:7; Matthew 24:14)

How to Live Your Covenant
"Embracing Lifestyle Surrender to Jesus"

As we draw to the close of this twenty-one day journey, it is not really an end but a new beginning! God calls you to the beginning of a new life under Christ's Lordship. At this juncture, a summary of Appendices A through E will provide a clear road map for your journey forward. Each appendix is a tool designed for a specific purpose and use. (In addition to being printed in this book, each appendix is available as a Bible insert card for ongoing use.) Please read the following basic descriptions of the various tools.

Appendix A contains **My Personal** and **Church Covenant to Return to God**. In addition to asking their members to embrace a personal covenant, many churches will publically commit to a "corporate covenant" for returning to God. Both of these covenants are printed on a Bible insert card for periodic reminder. **Appendices B** through **E** provide practical tools for implementing each point of the covenants.

Appendix B is entitled **My Covenant to Walk with God in Daily Cleansing**. This appendix is a concise, yet thorough, cleansing guide to experience full daily cleansing and yielding to Christ's Lordship. If modern saints are to walk in biblical power, deeper cleansing and yielding *must* become a greater part of quiet times! This tool is simple, yet powerful for consistent use. It is available as a laminated Bible insert.

Appendix C is entitled, **My Covenant to Daily Abide in God's Word and Prayer.** The tool is a biblical quiet time pattern that restores all the key elements of an effective daily prayer life. Sadly, many devotional patterns fall short of the biblical essentials for full empowerment. As a result, many Christians have gotten stuck at fairly basic (or low) levels of power and fullness. It is impossible to effectively "abide in Christ" if daily prayer patterns remain inadequate or overly rushed. **Appendix C** provides a biblical, relational prayer pattern that revolutionizes growth and power. Best of all, it is simple enough for any believer to experience God's closeness.

Appendix D is entitled, **My Great Commission Prayer Covenant.** This tool equips believers to effectively pray for lost people, missionaries, unreached people groups, struggling loved ones and key missions concerns. Evangelistic kingdom praying is vital for fully embracing Christ's Lordship. **My Great Commission Prayer Covenant** is available as a laminated Bible insert.

Appendix E is entitled, **My Covenant to Pray for Revival and Spiritual Awakening.** In this tool, believers learn to pray God's heart biblically, specifically and powerfully. By so doing, they become "co-laborers with God" for renewing the Church and turning today's rising tide of darkness. While we are not required to pray through these each day, even periodic prayer will make an enormous difference in lives and churches. By God's grace, *any* believer can use these practical tools for phenomenal closeness with God!

We Must Now Obey What We Know!

Each person who has read to this point, has a stronger understanding of full surrender to Jesus. You also have simple practical tools for ongoing closeness with God. The Lord has given the awesome gift of His Spirit and Word to help you walk in ever deepening power. He has provided tools so simple that the youngest believer could use them. But now we come to a crucial point. *It is time to act!* With knowledge and ability comes great accountability. With full knowledge and practical tools, there can be no excuse for business as usual. (Luke 12:47-48)

Friends, if revival could come by brief, surface quiet times and general confession, it would have long since done so. In today's world we must come to understand that our churches, families and nation really are at stake! But be assured — our God is both merciful and gracious to help us change. From this point forward, let us covenant to walk in revival fullness! Prayerfully read through Appendices A through E. By God's grace, we return to Him in empowered first love living! May God help us settle for nothing less.

The Appendices

Appendix A

My Covenant to Return to God
"The Pledge to Lasting, First Love Surrender"
(Psalm 27:8; Zechariah 1:3)

1. Father God, I renounce all lukewarmness and lack of spiritual passion. By Your grace and Spirit I covenant to love, revere and seek You with all my heart. I covenant to love my neighbor as myself and bless my enemies. (Ecclesiastes 12:13; Matthew 22:37-39)

2. Lord Jesus, I repent of all anger, impurity, lust and pride. By Your grace and Spirit, I covenant to walk with clean hands, a pure heart and godly attitudes for Your glory. (Matthew 5:8; John 13:34; 1 Peter 5:5)

3. Heavenly Father, I repent of all unforgiveness and broken relationships. By Your grace and Spirit, I pledge to seek forgiveness of all I have offended and fully forgive all who have offended me. (Matthew 5:23-24, 6:14-15, 18:35)

4. Blessed Savior, I repent of neglecting Your word and prayer. By Your grace and Spirit, I covenant to daily abide in Your word, prayer and spiritual fullness. (John 15:4-15; Ephesians 5:18)

5. Holy God, I repent of shallow confession and surface yielding of my life. By Your grace and Spirit, I covenant to walk in full repentance and ever-deeper yielding to Christ's Lordship. (Psalm 66:16; Luke 6:46)

6. Holy Father, I repent of lukewarmness in evangelism and missions. By Your grace and Spirit, I covenant to consistently give, labor and pray for lost people, missions and kingdom growth. (Matthew 28:18-20; Acts 1:8)

7. Sovereign Lord, I repent of my failure to pray and labor for revival and spiritual awakening. By Your grace and Spirit, I covenant to consistently pray for powerful revival in the Church, spiritual awakening and evangelistic harvest for Christ's eternal worship. (Psalm 85:6; Isaiah 43:7; Matthew 24:14)

Our Church Covenant to Return to God
(2 Chronicles 7:14; Psalm 139:23-24; Joel 2:12-13; Matthew 6:33, 22:37-39; John 15:4-5; 2 Corinthians 7:1; 1 Peter 4:17; Revelation 2:1-4, 22:20)

"Holy God, we humbly acknowledge our desperate need to return to You in full repentance and lasting first love passion. Please forgive us for rushed shallow prayer times, spiritual apathy and religious activities without power. Forgive us for emphasizing programs and strategies over fervent prayer, deep repentance and Great Commission passion. We understand that judgment "begins at the house of God" and that we are primarily responsible for the nation's spiritual condition.

Lord, we further understand that our prayers and repentance must become deep, specific and lasting, not brief and general. No longer will we merely "say" we repent. We know we must do more than give general lip service to prayer, repentance, evangelism and missions. By Your grace, we therefore covenant to promote four concrete steps of loving obedience in our members. (1) An initial full life examination and deep patterns of daily repentance thereafter, (2) Daily personal prayer times that are substantial and kingdom-focused, (3) Consistent prayer for and witnessing to specific lost people with significant prayer, giving and labor for missions, (4) Consistent prayer using the twelve biblical prayers for sweeping revival and spiritual awakening

Dear Savior by Your Spirit and grace alone, we fully commit to pray and obey Your heart as reflected in the covenant prayer guides, cleansing Scriptures and evangelistic tools in Return to Me. Whether our nation first sees revival or increasing judgment, we hereby covenant to seek Your face. Revive the Church O Lord. Send sweeping global harvest and glorify Your holy name. Come Lord Jesus, come quickly!" (Revelation 22:20)

Appendix B
My Covenant to Walk in Daily Cleansing and Yielding
"A Concise Guide to Personal Repentance and Yielding"

A Covenant Prayer – *"Lord and Savior, I covenant to walk with You in first love passion and obedience. I understand that loving You means ever-deeper cleansing and yielding of my heart. By Your grace, I therefore covenant to add cleansing and surrender as a frequent part of my daily prayer time. As your Spirit guides, I will allow Your full searching of all areas of my life."*

As believers embrace deeper daily cleansing, it is vital to remember three key truths. We are fully accepted in Christ's blood and righteousness. Let us keep our eyes on God's grace. God convicts to transform, not condemn His children. Do not just confess sins, also forsake them! (Proverbs 28:13) We gain victory by "putting on righteousness," not just putting off the sins. Believe Christ to live through you. In faith, simply ask Him to daily fill you with His Holy Spirit.

A Guide for Personal Confession

Seven Areas for Consistent Examination and Surrender

Pure Thoughts — *"For as he thinks in his heart, so is he."* (Proverbs 23:7a) Fully confess and forsake whatever sins God brings to mind. Trust God to fill and empower you with His Spirit. (a) Do I have any pattern of unclean or lustful thoughts? (b) Have I viewed anything that inflames wrong thoughts? (c) Do I think far more about worldly things than spiritual? (d) Am I often guilty of angry thoughts? (e) Do I frequently entertain thoughts of doubt instead of trust? (f) Am I often filled with thoughts of bitterness and unforgiveness? Put off sinful thoughts and put on Christ by faith. Believe Christ to live through you by the Holy Spirit. (Romans 6:11)

Godly Attitudes — *"Let this mind (*attitude*) be in you, which was also in Christ Jesus."* (Philippians 2:5) Fully confess and forsake any areas God brings to mind. Trust God to fill and empower you by His Spirit. (a) Am I lukewarm about spiritual things? (b) Am I in any way proud or condescending toward others? (c) Is there anyone about whom I think jealous, envious thoughts? (d) Do I have an attitude of doubt, fear or unbelief? (e) Do I have any tendency toward being harsh or critical? Put off wrong attitudes and let the mind of Christ dwell in you. Believe Christ to live through you by the Holy Spirit. (Romans 6:11)

Holy Speech and Cyberspace — *"Let no corrupt word proceed out of your mouth, but that which is good for necessary edification, that it may impart grace unto the hearers."* (Ephesians 4:29) *"in everything give thanks: for this is the will of God in Christ Jesus for you."* (1 Thessalonians 5:18) Fully confess and forsake any sins of speech. Trust God to fill and empower you by His Spirit. (a) Have I uttered any inappropriate or slang speech? (b) Do I have patterns of cursing or off-color words? (c) Am I prone to exaggeration or lying? (d) Do I have patterns of complaining and griping? (e) Have I spoken or emailed any form of divisive speech? (f) Do I have any patterns of critical, judgmental speech or emails? Put off all ungodly speech and yield your tongue to Christ's Lordship. Believe Christ to live through you by the Holy Spirit. (Romans 6:11)

Right Relationships — *"Therefore if you bring your gift to the altar, and there remember that your brother has something against you, leave your gift there before the altar, and go your way. First be reconciled to your brother, and then come and offer your gift.....For if you forgive men their trespasses, your heavenly Father will also forgive you. But if you do not forgive men their trespasses, neither will your Father forgive your trespasses."* (Matthew 5:23-24, 6:14-15) Fully confess and forsake all relationship sins. Take your time and be thorough! (a) Is there anyone I have offended but have not asked forgiveness? (b) Have I failed to seek full reconciliation and make restitution to anyone I have offended or harmed? (c) Do I harbor the slightest unforgiveness and anger toward anyone? (d) As a father, am

I leading my family spiritually? (e) As a mother, am I sacrificially and joyfully serving my family? (f) Have I in any way failed to honor, respect or show attention to my parents? (g) Have I spoken negatively about anyone behind their back? (h) Am I involved in any form of gossip or negative, critical speech or emails? (i) Have any of my social medial conversations become excessive or inappropriate? ___ (J) Is there any pattern of failing to respect and support my spiritual leaders? Put off sins of relationship and let Jesus be the Lord of all.

Rejecting Sins of Commission — *"For I acknowledge my transgressions; and my sin is ever before me."* (Psalm 51:3) Fully confess and forsake all sins of commission. (a) Am I engaged in any form of sexual immorality? (b) Have I compromised by viewing anything unclean via movies, TV or Internet? (c) Do I have habits that abuse or neglect my body? (d) Do I commit idolatry by placing anyone or anything over loving and serving God? (e) Have I dabbled in any form of gambling or new ageism? (f) Am I doing anything for which I do not have perfect peace? (g) Am I in any way harsh or unkind to others? (h) Have I abused God's grace by taking sin lightly? (i) Do I confess sins but fail to forsake them? Put off disobedience and put on full surrender to Christ.

Renouncing Sins of Omission — *"Therefore to him who knows to do good, and does not do it, to him it is sin."* (James 4:17) Fully confess and forsake any patterns of omission. (a) Am I failing to abide in Jesus by neglecting regular time in His word and prayer? (b) Do I neglect to be a daily witness and fail to generously support evangelism and missions? (c) Have I neglected to discern and use my spiritual gifts? (d) Am I allowing any point of spiritual bondage to remain in my life? (e) Have I in any way failed to support and respect my spiritual leaders? (f) Am I failing to daily pursue holiness? (g) Am I robbing God by failing to tithe and give generous offerings beyond the tithe? (h) Have I neglected to work at improving my marriage and family life? (i) Do I fail to pray with my family? Believe Christ to live through you by the Holy Spirit. (Romans 6:11) Put off sins of neglect and put on full obedience.

Embracing Full Surrender and Obedience to Jesus — *"If anyone desires to come after Me, let him deny himself and take up his cross, and follow Me.* (Matthew 16:24) Fully confess and forsake whatever God reveals in the following questions. (a) Have you willfully failed to surrender any part of your life to God's total control? (b) Has God told you to do something yet you still haven't obeyed Him? (c) Is there some area where you pretend not to know what God is saying, yet deep down you know you do? (d) Are there things God has told you to stop; yet you still do them? (e) Is there any area of service you should be doing; yet you are not? (f) Have you continued to sin willfully in areas about which God has clearly spoken? Believe Christ to live through you by the Holy Spirit. (Romans 6:11) Put off self-will and wholly surrender to Christ's Lordship.

(For further help and study on cleansing and repentance, use the book, **Returning to Holiness** by Gregory Frizzell.)

Appendix C

My Covenant to Abide Daily in God's Word and Prayer

A Covenant Prayer – *"Lord and Savior, I covenant to walk with You in first love passion and obedience. I understand that effective time in Your Word and prayer are crucial to living in fullness and power. As a love relationship by Your grace, I commit to embrace six steps as my ongoing pattern: (1) To regularly spend significant time in Your Word and prayer; (2) To seek to read through the Bible at least once each year; (3) To daily (or regularly) spend time in the four different types of prayer; (4) To focus my prayers on Your kingdom and glory; (5) To include cleansing of heart as a frequent part of my prayer times; (6) To embrace these patterns as a love relationship guided by Your Spirit, not a rigid formula."*

How to Daily Read and Meditate on God's Word

"Five Basics Steps"
(Do not view these five steps as a legalistic requirement. While these steps are important, they are not a rigid formula. Let God guide you in patterns and steps for each day.)

1. Embrace a Scripture reading plan that will take you through the entire Bible at least once each year. (Most Bibles have a reading plan listed in the back)

2. Use a quality study Bible that explains the historic context of each day's reading.

3. Before you read the Scriptures, always ask God to cleanse your heart and give you ears to hear His voice.

4. Try to keep a journal to record impressions of what God says to your heart.

5. As you read the Bible, the following questions will help you hear and apply what God is saying.

    a. What does today's reading tell me about God?

    b. Is there a sin or error I need to correct in my life?

    c. Is there an action I need to take?

    d. Is there a promise to claim or a truth to apply?

A Daily Pattern for Powerful Personal Prayer
(The following pattern is both biblical and thorough. However, it is not a legalistic requirement or rigid formula. You may or may not be led to pray daily through all the categories or in this order. Your prayer time is to be a Spirit-guided relationship, not a ritual or formula. Simply ask God to guide you from day to day.)

I. **Praise and Worship – Begin with a period of praise and thanksgiving (Spend a few minutes focusing on the glory and greatness of God. Hallow His holy name.)** Psalms 100:4-5

    ➤ Spend some time praising God for who He is (His characteristics and names)

    ➤ Take a few moments to thank God for past, present, and future blessings

    ➤ Take time just to freely worship and adore Him from your heart

II. **Repentance/Confession and Yielding – Continue with confession and repentance (at least 5 - 15 minutes)** Proverbs 28:13; Psalms 66:18, 139:23-24; 1 John 1:9

    ➤ Ask God to search your thoughts and attitudes

    ➤ Carefully examine your words and relationships

    ➤ Confess any sins of commission and forsake whatever God reveals

> Confess any sins of omission and make a definite commitment to obedience

> Ask God to fill you with the Holy Spirit

III. **Intercession/Protection/Deliverance** – **Proceed with Prayers of Intercession, Spiritual Warfare and Kingdom Advancement (10 - 20 minutes)** Ezekiel 22:30, Matthew 6:13; 2 Timothy 2:1-4

> Pray for needs of family and friends

> Pray for your pastor and church

> Pray for specific lost people by name

> Pray for spiritual protection and the removal of strongholds

> Pray for missionaries and mission efforts (Use guides from both the *International and North American Mission Boards*)

> Pray for revival and spiritual awakening in your church and nation

(In your intercession, remember the value of focusing on only two or three categories per day. If you thoroughly prayed for every category, you could literally pray for hours! Though some may be led to pray for hours, most people will focus on specific categories on certain days. As always, the guiding principle is close sensitivity to the Holy Spirit.)

IV. **Supplication/Petition** – **Move into Prayers of Personal Petition (10 - 15 minutes)** Philippians 4:6; Matthew 6:33

> Pray for the development of character and holiness. Strong options are to pray through the fruits of the Holy Spirit or other character words (Matthew 5:1-12; Galatians 5:22)

> Pray for guidance and power on your life, ministry and service to God (be very specific in your prayers)

> Pray for any physical, emotional, spiritual or financial needs

V. **Meditative Listening – Conclude with a Time of Scripture Meditation and Listening for God's Voice**

➢ Reflect on key points of your scripture reading and prayer time

➢ Assess how God has impressed on your heart

➢ Write down key impressions in a daily journal

➢ End your time with thanksgiving for God's grace, mercy, protection and power

The above pattern is a biblical, fully empowered relationship with Jesus. Again, I emphasize the above pattern is a general guideline, not a rigid program. As you allow God's Spirit to guide, you will be amazed at the ways He will direct you day by day. If we are willing, Jesus enables us to walk with Him in deep spiritual intimacy. Every believer can have a mountain-moving prayer life. May God help us settle for nothing less than the glory of His manifest presence!

(For personal growth and group studies on powerful prayer, use the book, *How to Develop a Powerful Prayer Life,* by Gregory Frizzell.)

Appendix D

My Great Commission Prayer Covenant
"Praying for Lost People and Missions"

"The effective, fervent prayer of the righteous is powerful."
(James 5:16b)

A Covenant Prayer – *"Lord and Savior, I desire to walk with You in first love passion and obedience. I understand that a vital part of loving You is to obey Your Great Commission. Because You have commanded us to witness to all the world and make disciples, **I covenant to do five things**. (1) I will abide in Christ's power by daily cleansing, fullness and prayer. (2) I will pray for myself and my church to have a strong missional focus and witness to all the world. (3) I will fervently pray for my list of lost souls and ever seek ways to bring them to Christ. (4) I will seek to love, serve and witness to others wherever I go. (5) Lord, by Your grace, I will pray fervently, give sacrificially and labor continually for specific local and global missions."*

People I Covenant to Lift to God

_____

_____

_____

_____

Biblical Prayers for Lost People, Wayward Believers and Loved Ones in Bondage

✝ Pray for God to *deeply convict* of their personal sin and lostness (Acts 2:37; John 16:8)

✝ Pray for God to *fully open their eyes* and *reveal Christ* as Lord and Savior (Matthew 16:17; 2 Corinthians 4:4)

✝ Pray for God to powerfully *draw them to Christ* by the Holy Spirit (John 6:44)

✝ Pray for God to *tear down strongholds* that are keeping them from salvation or full surrender. (2 Corinthians 10:3-5) Ask God for insight into their strongholds and pray specifically for their removal.

✝ Pray for God to make their hearts *good soil fully receptive* to Christ (Matthew 13:8)

✝ Pray for God to move them to *new birth, saving faith* and *true repentance* (2 Corinthians 5:17; Luke 13:3; Ephesians 2:8-9)

✝ Pray that they *become fruitful disciples* and *witnesses* that lead others to Christ (Matthew 28:18-20; John 15:8)

(For information on how to give an effective personal witness, check out www.My316.com)

Specific Missions Needs I Will Lift to God

Adopted People Groups – _____

_____

Adopted Missionaries/Projects–_____

_____

Strategies and Specific Needs – _____

_____

Praying Around the World Project – use free guide from__ "Operation World" — www.operationworld.org_____

Biblical Prayers for Missionaries and Mission Concerns

† Pray for *great empowerment, provision* and *protection* for missionaries and their families. (Acts 1:8; Philippians 4:19; Ephesians 6:13)

† Pray for the God's word *to run swiftly* and have *free course*. (2 Thessalonians 3:1)

† Pray for *wisdom and empowerment* in all evangelism, discipleship and missions strategies. (James 1:5)

† Pray for Satan and evil forces to be *restrained, truth revealed* and *strongholds demolished*. (2 Corinthians 10:3-5)

† Pray for *overwhelming conviction, spiritual drawing, revelation* and *salvation* to sweep the nations. (John 16:8; Acts 2:37; Ephesians 1:17-19)

† Pray for *strong discipleship* of converts and the *raising up* of church planters, preachers, teachers and witnesses. (Matthew 9:38, 28:18-20)

† Pray for great *encouragement, grace, power, protection* and *provision* for persecuted saints. (John 17:15; Philippians 4:19; 2 Thessalonians 2:16-17)

† Pray for God's *glory to be revealed, His Name* to be *praised* and *Christ's kingdom to explode* throughout the earth.

(For daily updates on missions needs, log on to www.imb.org and www.namb.net and select Prayer Request. For updates on persecuted saints go to www.persecution.com.)

Appendix E

My Covenant to Pray for Revival and Spiritual Awakening

Effective prayer for revival and spiritual awakening is God's will for every believer. In fact, such prayer is the only real hope for our land! Yet, the prayers that bring sweeping revival are not casual or general. The twelve prayers in this covenant are unique in that they cover all key elements of true revival and church vitality. While they are not rote formulas to repeat verbatim, they do represent much of God's heart and kingdom purpose. Believers, it is time for our prayers to deepen, our understanding to increase and our hearts to fully align with God's. Let us covenant to make the following prayers key elements in personal quiet times and corporate prayer meetings. *"The effective fervent prayer of a righteous man avails much."* James 5:16

My Covenant Prayer – *"Lord and Savior, I covenant to walk with You in first love passion and obedience. Father, I understand that Your heart is focused on reviving the Church and sending spiritual awakening to a lost world. Therefore by Your grace, I covenant to embrace Your heart for revival and awakening in three ways: (1) As the Holy Spirit guides, I will pray through the Twelve Biblical Prayers for Revival and Spiritual Awakening; (2) I will take time to initially study through the twelve prayers to sensitize my heart to Your kingdom priorities; (3) I will urge my church and small groups to periodically pray through The Twelve Biblical Prayers for Revival and Spiritual Awakening."* Be encouraged — *"the effective, fervent prayer of a righteous man does avail much!*

Twelve Biblical Prayers for Revival and Spiritual Awakening

1. **Plead for God's Merciful Grace on a Nation and Many Churches that are Under His Righteous Judgment** (2 Chronicles 7:14; Psalm 85:4-7; Daniel 9:18-19; Hebrews 4:16; James 4:8-10; 1 Peter 4:17)

2. **Cry Out for Deep Brokenness, Godly Fear and Humble Repentance to Sweep God's People** (Psalm 51:17; Proverbs 28:13; John 14:15; 2 Corinthians 7:1,10; Ephesians 5:26-27; Hebrews 12:14)

3. **Pray for an Explosion of First Love Passion for Christ and a Deep Burden for Lost Humanity** (Matthew 5:6, 44, 22:37-39; Philippians 2:13; 1 John 4:7-11, 20-21; Revelation 2:1-4, 3:15)

4. **Cry Out for a Mighty Movement of Fervent Personal and Corporate Prayer with Spirit-led Fasting** (2 Chronicles 7:14; Joel 1:14, 2:12-18; Matthew 6:16-18, 17:21, 21:13; Mark 11:17; Acts 2:1, 4:30-31; James 5:16)

5. **Plead for God's Powerful Manifest Presence, a Restraining of Evil and a Mighty Outpouring of His Spirit** (Exodus 33:15; 1 Kings 8:11; Isaiah 59:19; Zechariah 4:6; Acts 1:8, 2:1-2, 4:31)

6. **Pray for a Burning Passion for Evangelism, Discipleship and Missions to Sweep God's People** (Matthew 24:14, 28:18-20; Luke 19:10; Acts 1:8; Romans 9:1-3)

7. **Plead for Church Leaders to be Filled with Holy Boldness, Fervent Prayer, Spiritual Power and Strong Scripture Focus** (1 Timothy 3:1-2; 2 Timothy 1:6-7; 1 Corinthians 2:4)

8. **Cry Out for Supernatural Love and Unity to Sweep Churches, Denominations and Families** (John 13:34-35, 15:12, 17:20-22; Acts 2:1, 42-47; 1 Corinthians 1:10; Ephesians 4:29-32)

9. **Pray for Powerful Faith, Pure Motives and Godly Wisdom in Seasons of Judgment** (Joshua 1:9; Jeremiah 29:16-18, 45:5; Acts 4:29-31; Matthew 6:33, 9:29, 16:18, 17:20; Mark 9:23, 11:22-24; 2 Timothy 1:7; James 4:1-4)

10. **Plead for Churches to Fully Proclaim Christ's Preeminence, Calvary's Cross and True New-Birth Conversion** (John 3:3, 13:32, 16:8-14; Acts 4:12; Romans 6:1-14; Philippians 2:5-11; Colossians 1:9-18)

11. **Cry Out for an Explosion of Sound Biblical Doctrine and Theology with Full Exaltation of God's Glory and Grace** (1 Chronicles 29:10-13; Isaiah 42:8; Acts 20:27; 1 Corinthians 1:29; Ephesians 1:3-6, 2:7-9; 1 Timothy 1:17)

12. **Plead for God to Rend the Heavens in Sweeping Revival and to Transform the Nations in Spiritual Awakening. Cry Out for Christ's Swift Return!** (Psalm 2:8, 72:11, 85:6-7; Isaiah 64:1; Acts 2:1-2, 4:30-31; Ephesians 5:26-27; Revelations 22:17, 20) (For further help and study, use **Forty Days of Seeking God** and or **Praying God's Heart in Times Like These** by Gregory Frizzell.

Scripture References

Old Testament

Psalms

Proverbs

Ecclesiastes

Isaiah

New Testament

Mark

Luke

John

2 Corinthians

Galatians

Ephesians

Philippians

Colossians

1 Thessalonians

2 Thessalonians

End Notes

1. Frizzell, Gregory, *Praying for Revival, Elections and Key Leaders*, (Baptist General Convention of Oklahoma, 2008) 14.

2. Frizzell, Gregory, *Praying God's Heart in Times Like These*, (Baptist General Convention of Oklahoma, 2009) 23.

3. Stanford, Miles, *The Reckoning That Counts*, (Zondervan, 1977) 19.

4. Roberts, Richard, *Repentance: The First Word of the Gospel,* (Crossway Books, 2002) 130.

5. Thomas, Ian, *The Indwelling Life of Christ*, (Multnomah Books, 2006) 101.

6. Liederbach, Mark and Alvin Reid, *The Convergent Church: Missional Worshipers in an Emerging Culture*, (Kregel, 2009) 89.

7. Tozer, A. W., *The Attributes of God, Volume 2*, (Wing Spread Publishing, 2001) 44.

8. Ingram, Chip, *God as He Longs for You to See Him*, (Baker Books, 2004) 14.

9. Frizzell, Gregory, *Returning to Holiness: A Personal and Churchwide Journey to Revival,* (The Master Design Publisher, 2000) 21.

10. Strong, James, *The Strongest Strong's Exhaustive Concordance of the Bible*, (Zondervan, 201) 1603.

11. Frizzell, Gregory, *Releasing the Revival Flood*, (The Master Design Publisher, 2005) 43.

12. Frizzell, *Returning to Holiness,* 27.

13. Platt, David, *Radical: Taking Back Your Faith from the American Dream,* (Multnomah Books, 2010) 113.

14. *Urban Dictionary http//www.urbandictionary.com* (Snark) March 9, 2009

15. Strong, James, *The Strongest Strong's Exhaustive Concordance of the Bible*, (Zondervan, 201) 1653.

16. Jones, Sheila, *A Christian Parent's Checklist,* sjonesaz@ aol.com.

17. Frizzell, Gregory, Powerful Prayer for Every Family: Prayers That Protect and Transform, (Baptist General Convention of Oklahoma, 2005) 2.

18. Frizzell, *Returning to Holiness,* 52.

19. Hunt, T.W., *The Life-changing Power of Prayer*, (Broadman Holman, 2005) 4.

20. Frizzell, Gregory, *Personal and Church Survey Research of Spiritual Life; Measuring by God's Word, not Ourselves*, (Baptist General Convention of Oklahoma, 2012)

Returning to Holiness: *"A Personal and Churchwide Journey to Revival"*

A Companion Book for "Return to Me"

For those who want to read a sequel to **Return to Me**, a powerful option is **Returning to Holiness**. This book has similarities to **Return to Me** but addresses additional areas of surrender and growth. It also deals with salvation and full assurance. The book was 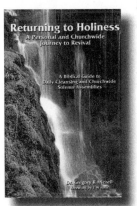 actually published in the year 2000 and soon expanded into nearly forty languages with well over a million copies in print. **Return to Holiness** has been usually blessed of God.

With no promotion, it continues to expand with ever-growing impact. The Scripture-filled resource brings readers into far deeper intimacy with God. As a result, the power of the Spirit becomes much more real in daily life. It is equally powerful for individuals, small groups or church-wide studies. Through this tool, a host of churches have experienced revival and many thousands have found Christ as their Savior.

How to Develop a Powerful Prayer Life: *"The Biblical Path to Holiness and Relationship with God"*

Another companion book is **How to Develop a Powerful Prayer Life**. In a way that is practical and Scripture-filled, readers re-capture key missing elements to biblical power in prayer.

Unfortunately, a troubling percentage of today's prayer models leave out at least two elements of deepest intimacy and power in Christ. In **How to Develop a Powerful Prayer Life**, readers experience all elements of mountain-moving prayer. Yet they learn to experience prayer as a Spirit-guided "relationship," not some rigid program or formula. This tool has evidenced an unusual blessing of God. Without promotion or advertising, the tool  is approaching a million copies in print. It is in an ever-expanding number of languages.

Upcoming New Release!

How to Pray Without Ceasing: *"The Power of Talking and Listening To God All the Time"*

Another sequel book is **How to Pray Without Ceasing**. This tool covers practical ways to talk and listen to God throughout the day. Because prayer is far beyond just the quiet time, it is vital for believers to learn to stay tuned into God continuously. It is also crucial to be able to fully discern God's direction and wisdom.

How to Pray
Without Ceasing

"The Power of Talking and
Listening to God All Day"

Learn to Clearly Hear God's Voice

The Joy of Walking with Jesus

Gregory Reed Frizzell

In a day of unprecedented deception and distraction, it has never been more critical to be able to *clearly* hear God's voice! In addition to clear spiritual hearing, **How to Pray Without Ceasing** helps believers walk in the flow and power of the Holy Spirit. This tool addresses key foundations frequently missing in modern believers and leaders. It covers areas often neglected in modern churches. The resource is equally effective for individuals, small groups and church-wide studies.

Iceberg Dead Ahead: *"The Urgency of God-Seeking Repentance"*

A fourth suggested resource is the pilot version of **Iceberg Dead Ahead**. Released in the fall of 2007, its timing was very significant. It preceded a devastating series of societal and spiritual "icebergs" by only four months. The book clearly outlines the severity of today's economic, moral and spiritual collapse. More importantly, it addresses *why* the collapse has occurred and *how* God brings churches and nations back to Himself. The tool is powerful for laymen and leaders alike.

Iceberg Dead Ahead!
The Urgency of "God-Seeking Repentance"

Learning to Seek God in the Face of Judgment

Restoring the "Relational Foundations" of Revival

Dr. Gregory Frizzell

The updated final version is slated for release in mid to late 2013. In the meantime, this book has unique relevance to modern believers and churches. But far from being defeatist or negative, readers are strengthened in their hope of God's faithfulness and power. Believers are equipped to be victorious whether the future brings revival or worsening judgments.